COMING INTO FREEDOM

EMILIE CADY'S LESSONS IN TRUTH FOR THE 21ST CENTURY

RUTH L. MILLER, PH.D.

WISEWOMAN PRESS

Coming into Freedom: Emilie Cady's Lessons in Truth for the 21st Century

WiseWoman Press
Portland, OR

www.wisewomanpress.com

ISBN: 978-0-945385-23-3

PREFACE

Charles Fillmore was looking for a clear explanation of the basic principles he had learned from his teacher, Emma Curtis Hopkins, when his wife Myrtle handed him a pamphlet called "Finding the Christ in Ourselves" by a doctor in New York, H. Emilie Cady. The Fillmores agreed that this was indeed someone who both understood and practiced the principles they were teaching, and Charles invited her to prepare a series of articles for his magazine, a predecessor of today's *Unity*.

Dr. Cady complied and reprints of her articles were so frequently requested that they were constantly rolling off Charles' presses. Finally, he combined them into two little booklets of six articles each. Later, he combined the two into one, numbering the paragraphs to make it easier for groups to read it together.

That Dr. Cady was not pleased with this editing of her work is made clear in a letter published as the introduction of a later work, *How I Used Truth*. Nonetheless, Charles persisted, and *Lessons in Truth* remains the foundation text for all churches and classes in the Unity Association today, over a hundred years later.

Harriet Emilie Cady, like many single women of the Suffrage era, including Mary Baker Eddy, the founder of Christian Science, was a homeopathic physician during the mid- to late 1800s. This was the time when the science of metaphysics was just being discovered in this country, primarily through the work of Phineas Quimby and his followers, including Mrs. Eddy.

Several of Mrs. Eddy's early students had struck out on their own; among them, Emma Curtis Hopkins. She ran a seminary in Chicago and one of her first students introduced the Fillmores to the science. She also lectured in other cities, including New York, where Dr. Cady encountered her unique presentation. A good deal of the content of *Lessons* closely parallels those lectures, though Dr. Cady definitely imprinted her distinctive stamp on them.

The King James Bible was her primary spiritual source, and she included many biblical quotations in her lessons. Likewise, Victorian rhetoric was her writing style. Between the two, unfortunately, many students today have difficulty with the language of the lessons, and this has kept them from experiencing the power of her ideas.

So the following pages are a "transliteration" of Cady's original text into modern usage. I've taken the liberty of simplifying the sentences, "translating" some of her terms, replacing some of the examples with more modern ones, and re-organizing some of the text—always with an eye to maintaining the essential meaning.

It's always enlightening to do this sort of work with writers of the caliber of Hopkins, Waddles, and Cady. I find their practical understanding of the esoteric principles deepens mine every time.

May you, too, find the power of Truth that Emilie Cady has shown so many.

rlm

CONTENTS

LESSON ONE: SLAVERY OR FREEDOM— WHICH?

As you begin this course, please put aside all your previous ideas, beliefs, or actions. By "suspending disbelief" you'll find it easier to take in what is being offered. You won't be, as Luke said, putting "new wine into old wineskins" (Luke 5:37).[1] If you find, as we go along, something that you don't understand or agree with, just let it go until you've finished the entire course. Many things that disturb you at first will be made clear later on. Of course, after you've finished, you're free to go back to your old ways of thinking and believing. But for the time being, remember what the Master Jesus said: "except ye ... become as little children, ye shall in no wise enter into the kingdom of Heaven" (Matthew 18:3). Also, when you find things repeated, please remember that these are lessons, not lectures or essays.

OF HUMAN BONDAGE

Because of the things we were taught growing up and see in the media every day, each and every one of us believes that our life experience is determined by our bodies and the material world around us—and all of our suffering is the result of this belief. If we look at the Old Testament, though, we can read, in the story of Israel coming out of Egypt, the description of human consciousness moving up out of bondage in the physical, into the freedom of the spiritual.

> And Jehovah said (speaking to Moses) "I have surely seen the affliction of my people that are in Egypt, and have heard their cries by reason of their taskmasters, for I know their sorrows and I am come down to deliver them out of that land unto a good land and a large land, unto a land flowing with milk and honey" (Exodus 3:7, 8).

---

[1] New wine, as it ferments, expands. Old wineskins may be empty, but they are no longer flexible, so they crack and break under the pressure of the expanding new wine.

1

These words express exactly how the Creator feels toward humanity, today. Today and everyday our God has been saying to each and every one of us:

> I have surely seen the affliction of you who are in the darkness of ignorance and materialism, and have heard you cry because of your taskmasters: sickness, sorrow, and poverty. So I am (not *I will*, but *I am now*) come to deliver you out of all this suffering, and to bring you into a life of joy, comfort, and freedom.

COMING INTO FREEDOM

Sometime, somewhere, every one of us must come to our true Self. Like the Prodigal Son, having tired of eating cornhusks, each of us will "arise and go to my Father" (Luke 15:18). And we will do so in all humility and praise, as it is written, "The Lord says, before me every knee shall bow" (Romans 14:11).

This doesn't mean that God is a stern autocrat compelling us to bow before Him. Rather, it's a description of the order, the law, of the universe: the law of All-love, All-good.

Humanity, at first living in our physical self-centered, animal nature, will grow up, stage by stage, to the spiritual understanding that we are one with the creative force of the universe. At that point we are free from all suffering, because we realize that we have conscious dominion over all things.

And somewhere on this journey, our consciousness comes to a place where our hearts are full of joy and wonder. Then, gladly, we bow before the greatness of the Spirit working through us and around us. From that point on, with joyful freedom, our hearts cry out, "Alleluia! Hooray!" Everyone must sooner or later come to this experience.[2] This is the law.

You and I, dear Reader, have begun to wake up. We have become aware of the bondage of our past ignorance and have set out from our personal "Egypt" to our own "Paradise," the land of our liberty—and now we couldn't turn back if we wanted to. Yes, there may be times on our journey when we come into a deep wilderness or against a Red Sea and our courage may fail us. Yet, as

---

[2] Another great text, *A Course in Miracles*, says "...it is a required course. Only the time you take it is voluntary" (preface).

Moses said to the troubled Israelites, "Fear not; stand still and see the salvation which Jehovah shall work for you today" (Exodus 14:13).

Each of us must sooner or later stand alone with our god. Nothing else works. Nothing else will ever make you master of your own destiny.

AN INSIDE JOB

We've believed we were helped and comforted by others, that we received our joy from circumstances outside us, but that's not so. *All joy and strength and good come from inside,* and if we only knew this truth, we would see that *nothing outside of us can ever take away our joy or our good.*

Your own indwelling Spirit provides all the life and health, all the strength, peace, and joy, all the wisdom and support that you can ever need or desire. No one can give to you as this indwelling Presence can; it's the spring of all joy, comfort, and power.

HEIRS TO THE KINGDOM

Most of us have believed ourselves to be slaves (or victims) of circumstances. Some have said that, at best, we are servants of the Most High. Neither belief is true.

It's time for us to wake up fully, to know that we are not slaves, not servants, but sons and daughters, "and if children, then heirs," as Paul says in his letter to the Roman Christians (Romans 8:17).

Heirs to what? Heirs to all wisdom, so we need never make mistakes. Heirs to all love, so we need never feel fear, envy, or jealousy. Heirs to all strength, all power, all life, all good.

We're so used to the sound of the words we heard as children, that we often forget to look for the meaning in them. Have you ever considered what it means to be "heirs of God, and joint heirs with Christ?" It means, as Ralph Waldo Emerson said in the opening to his lesson on *History,* that "every[one] is the inlet, and may become the outlet, for all that is in God." It means that *all that God is and has is truly ours, the rightful heirs, if only we can claim our inheritance.*

3

So, in this course, we'll be learning how to claim that inheritance in our daily life.

Paul told the Christians in Galatia,

> So long as the heir is a child, he is no different from a bondservant, though he is lord of all; he is under guardians and stewards until the day appointed by his father. So we also, when we were children [in understanding], were held in bondage under the rudiments of the world. But ... the fullness of time came ... and because you are sons, God sent the Spirit of his Son into our hearts, crying "*Abba*, Father," so that you are no longer a bondservant, but a son; and if a son, then an heir through God. (Galatians 4:1-7)

The "Spirit of his Son" is the consciousness of the risen Christ that dwells in each of us. And it is through that indwelling Christ that we are to receive all that God has and is—as much or as little as we can (or dare to!) claim.

No matter what you thought started you on this journey, it was really because the "fullness of time" had come for you to claim your inheritance. You could no longer be satisfied with, or enslaved by, the material world.

The "fullness of time" for you is Now. It's time for you to be free, to have dominion over the material world, to no longer be a servant, but a firstborn heir to the kingdom—in full possession of your inheritance!

Yet, even as we take in that wonderful truth, we realize that if we're simply to claim what is ours, then we're no longer to look for rewards, or even a belief to follow. We're not to use this journey to get something, or to follow someone, but to find a new way to live life.

And in the course of these Lessons, we'll take the first steps toward that new life—a life of freedom, perfect love, and all good.

THE INNER LIFE, THE SECRET TO POWER

As we begin the journey, we discover that every loving thought that we think, every unselfish word or action, *must*, by an unchanging law, lead to good results for us. But, on the way, we learn not to focus on these results. Instead, we discover that we

4

must learn to *be* the Truth, consciously.[3] We realize that our power lies in learning to *consciously be* the love, the wisdom, the life that we already are in Truth (though not always consciously), and letting the results take care of themselves.

We bring these qualities into our consciousness by taking time alone, focusing on the Presence within us. *In daily meditation lies the secret of power.* No one can grow in spiritual knowledge or power without it. No one would dream of becoming a master musician or star basketball player without daily practice! You need to practice the Presence just as you would practice sports or music.

You may be so busy working, or even helping others, that it seems as if there's no time to go off by yourself. But the invitation is clear, "Come ye yourselves apart ... and rest awhile" (Mark 6:31). And it's the only way to gain definite knowledge, true wisdom, steady purpose, or even the power to meet the unknowns of daily life—the power that sets us free.

So if you've believed you don't have time for quiet meditation, make time; take time. If you look carefully, you'll find some things that might be better left undone. You may spend time watching tv, or gaming, or chatting with friends, that could be more usefully spent "refueling" in the silence, rather than diffusing your energy with other peoples' ideas.

Even some unselfish act may not be so important that you should neglect regular, daily meditation. The thing to remember is that *doing* is secondary to *being*. When we are consciously *being* the Truth, it radiates from us and does the work without our running around looking busy.

When you withdraw from the world into the silence, don't think about yourself, your challenges, your old dreams, or your failures. Let all the old fears and troubles go for a while. Work at turning your thoughts away from them. Never let your minutes or hours apart be spent in effort or concern, but always experience them as your time of peace—just calm, quiet awakening, alone with the Presence within.

---

[3] A popular quote from the leader of India's independence movement, Mohandas (Mahatma) Gandhi, is: "Be the change you wish to see in the world."

Focus on God. *Let all of your thoughts center on the nature of the Creator and Sustainer of the universe.* If necessary, use the words of an old hymn or psalm, a familiar prayer, or a statement of Truth from this book to help shift your thoughts.

Until you've tried it, you'll never know how this simple practice quiets the nerves, reduces fears, and dissolves the stresses of the day into nothing.[4]

And, once you *have* tried it, you may be tempted to make the mistake of withdrawing from the world to spend all your time in meditation. This asceticism is neither wise nor profitable. We go inside to receive new life, new inspiration, new power, new supply from the overflowing fountain within, and then we return to the world around us to share that life and power in love. The life of Jesus, who showed us the Way, helps us to see this; each day he went off by himself, and each day he returned to share, renewed in Spirit and in power. So we, too, can go into the stillness each day, and come back into everyday life with new inspiration, courage, and power, for our good and the good of all.

Whenever anyone practices this daily Presence, peace and harmony flow through and fill not only the person, but also the surroundings. They reach into our home and workplace—in all the world around us, wherever we are. So you need not let concerns about others stop you; you are doing the very best you can for them, from the inside out.

BEING PEACE

As we experience this new clarity and power, it's important to remember that no one is so grand, so godlike, as one who, knowing the Truth, can stand meekly and unperturbed before the accusations of others—especially if they're false. Again, we remember Jesus, of whom it was prophesied, "Your gentleness has made me

---

[4] Many studies of meditation have shown that people who simply relax their bodies and focus on their breathing can reduce blood pressure, slow the pulse, and restore healthy function to the organs. A summary of the physical and emotional effects of meditation can be found in *Calm Healing: Methods for a New Era of Medicine* by Robert Bruce Newman and Ruth L. Miller.

great" (II Samuel. 22:36). Just as Jesus stood meekly, saying nothing, before the false accusations of Pontius Pilate, we need to live that quality of love and acceptance in our daily life.[5]

We find we must also forgive as we would be forgiven. Now, to forgive does *not* mean being indifferent to those who injure us. To forgive is really to give *for*—to give some actual definite good in return for the distress we've experienced. If you're like most people, you may be thinking, "I've got no one to forgive!" Yet, if we consider all the people we feel negatively about, or we think, "served him right," then we find we have much to forgive. Any pain you suffer, any failure of some expected good, is a useful indicator. It shows a remnant of unforgiveness you're holding— toward someone in particular, the world in general, or, for some, the power they call God. It's time to give love and acceptance instead of that negative feeling you've been sending their way.

Past beliefs about our circumstances or environment must be released, as well. No matter how ugly or evil circumstances may appear, or how much it may seem that someone else is the cause of sorrow or trouble, God's good, and that alone, is all that is truly there. So we release the memory, along with any feelings attached to it, as we forgive those involved. Joseph, sold by his brothers into slavery in Egypt, told them later, "you meant evil against me, but God meant it for good" (Genesis. 50:20). If we have the courage to see only the Truth of love and good in all, then even the "wrath of man" is turned to our advantage. Situations that seemed heartbreaking turn to joy before our very eyes—when we steadfastly refuse to see anything but God in them.

Finally, while it's perfectly natural for the human mind to seek to escape from troubles by running away from a situation or planning to make some physical changes, such attempts are foolish. *There is no real or permanent physical way to escape from circumstances or feelings;* all our help must come from within. The real inner consciousness that "The Lord is my shepherd; I shall not want"[6]

---

[5] And, again, the words and actions of Gandhi, as he led India's nonviolent revolution, are useful models.

[6] In this context the word "want" means "lack for," or "have to do without" anything. So another translation of this psalm could be:

(Psalm 23) will supply all needs more surely (and more liberally!) than any human hand. The felt understanding that "God is my defense and deliverance," which we begin to have when we hold the words in the silence until they become part of our inner being, will free anyone from the arguments of the smartest lawyer or most aggressive enforcer, in the world.

FOLLOWING THE WAY

Our ultimate goal must be to come into full awareness of the indwelling power of God, and then, in all circumstances, affirm our support, supply, and safety through and by this One. We don't need to run around, "helping" the divine do its work, but simply to hold a calm, restful, unwavering trust that the All-Wisdom and All-Power within us is able to bring about whatever is needed, always. When that victory is won—in the silence of our own being—then we don't ever need to do anything outwardly to relieve any situation.

David, as he was being hunted in the desert by his jealous king (who was also his father-in-law!), wrote:

I will lift my eyes to the heights,

Where my help is coming from.[7]

My help is from Yahweh,[8]

Who made Heaven and earth.

Yahweh will keep you from all evil …

From this time forward and forevermore (Psalm 121).

"The Spirit of Life within everything is caring for me, so I never have to do without anything that is good for me."

[7] This is often translated as a question: "whence cometh my help?" or "where is my help coming from?" Since written Hebrew has no punctuation, we don't know which is correct, but both work.

[8] The words "THE LORD" in small caps in the Bible were inserted wherever the translators found the Hebrew "tetragrammaton," which is the 4 letters that make the name of the Jewish God: JHVH. Most Jews believe that they must never speak that name, so they either blocked it out in their texts or replaced it with *Adonai*, which means "Lord." The most accurate pronunciation of the 4 letters appears to be *Yahweh*.

If only we could realize that this mighty power to save and protect, to deliver and make alive lives forever *within* us! Then perhaps we could stop, forever, looking to others!

Fortunately, there is a way to fully realize it: the way of the Christ Spirit. "I am the Way, the Truth, and the Life," are words said by Spirit through the risen master, Jesus (John 14). Holding onto the words "Christ is the Way; Christ lives in me" will always open the way to complete freedom.

SUMMARY

- Each and every one of us believes (to some extent at least) that our life experience is determined by our bodies and the material world around us, and all of our suffering is the result of this belief—not the conditions.

- Likewise, all joy and strength and good come from inside, and if we only knew this truth, we would see that nothing outside of us can ever take away our joy or our good.

- In daily meditation lies the secret of power: no one can grow in spiritual knowledge or power without some time each day focusing on the nature and reality of the Creative Source of All that Is.

- All human beings, at first living in our physical self-centered, animal nature, will grow up, stage by stage, to the spiritual understanding that we are one with the creative force of the universe.

- When we are consciously being the Truth, it radiates from us and does the work without our running around looking busy.

LESSON TWO: GOD, MAN, AND BEING

When Jesus was talking with the Samaritan woman at the well, He said to her "God is Spirit and they that worship Him must worship in spirit and truth" (John 4:24). Webster's dictionary definition of spirit says "life or consciousness viewed as an independent type of existence; one manifestation of the divine nature; the Holy Spirit."[9] We can't see spirit with our physical eyes, but when we look with our "sixth sense," or intuitive eyes, then spirit is visible and we recognize it. Similarly, you don't see the living, thinking "me" when you look with your eyes at my body; you see only the form I am manifesting at this time.

God, then, is not—as many of us have been taught to believe—"the big man in the sky," some gray-bearded person who lives in some beautiful region above the earth called "heaven" where people go when they die.[10] Nor is God a stern, angry judge, waiting for the chance to punish people who failed to live a perfect life here on earth.

God is not a person *having* life, intelligence, power, or love. God *is* that invisible, intangible, but very real something we *call* life. God is perfect love and infinite power. God is *the total* of these, the total of all good, both manifested and unexpressed.

God is Spirit, the invisible life and intelligence underlying all physical things, the creative energy that is the cause of all visible reality. *There is only one God in the universe, only one source of all the different forms of life or intelligence that we see:* animals, plants, human beings, microorganisms, water, and even rocks. As Plato put it, there could be no body, no visible reality, unless there is first Spirit as creative cause.[11]

---

9 The American Standard Version of the 1990s reads, "God is a spirit," but the note is "God is spirit" and other versions say "God is Spirit."

10 For a remarkable alternative view of the form and nature of God, see the novel, *The Shack,* by William Young.

11 Plato's view, that the forms we perceive are shadows of an ideal essence, is called "Platonism" among the schools of philosophy,

God is love. We cannot see love, nor even comprehend what love is, except as love in action. All the love in the universe is God. The love between husband and wife, or between parents and children, is just the smallest bit of God's love, as made manifest in visible form. A mother's true love, so infinitely tender, so unfailing, is God's love manifested a little through the mother.

God is wisdom and intelligence. All the wisdom and intelligence that we see in the universe is God: wisdom projected through a visible form. Up to now, we've looked for knowledge and help outside ourselves, not knowing that the source of all knowledge, the very spirit of truth and wisdom, is waiting within each and every one of us. To educate (from the Latin, *educare*, to lead forth) does *not* mean to force knowledge in from the outside, but always *to draw out from* the student something that already exists there. God as infinite wisdom lies within every human being, only waiting to be led forth into physical manifestation. Understanding and working with this awareness is true education.

God is power. Not simply God *has* power, but God *is* all the power that can do anything in this universe. God, as the creative energy that causes all visible reality, is the power that sustains and evolves this reality.

God is not a being having good qualities, but God is the good itself. God, the source of our existence in every moment. God is not only omnipotent (all-powerful), God is omnipotence (all power). God is not merely omniscient (all-knowing), God is omniscience (all wisdom, knowledge, and intelligence) itself. God is not merely omnipresent (always and everywhere present), God is more—omnipresence: everything you can think of, in its absolute perfect form, is God.

THE NATURE OF SUBSTANCE

God, then, is the substance (from the Latin *sub*, under, and *stare*, to stand), or the real thing standing under every visible form of life, intelligence, or power. Each rock, tree, or animal—every visible thing—is a manifestation of the one Spirit, God, varying

---

and Cady, along with the rest of the Unity and New Thought movement, is considered a "neo-Platonist."

only in degree. And *each one* of the infinite forms of manifestation, however insignificant, *contains the whole.* One drop of water taken from the ocean is just as perfect ocean water as is the whole: the molecules are the same, combined in exactly the same way, whether we consider a pail-full, a keg-full, or the entire ocean. Each is complete in itself; they differ only in quantity. Each contains the whole, yet nobody would make the mistake of confusing a drop with the entire ocean!

So we say that each individual form, or manifestation of God, contains the whole.

We don't for a moment mean that each individual person or rock is God in the entirety, but that each is God taking form in some degree or quantity.

God is not only the creative cause of every visible form at its beginning, but at every moment that form exists. God lives within every created thing as the life, the ever-renewing, re-creating, ever-evolving, cause of it. *God never is and never can be separated from any created form—not for a moment!* Then how can even a sparrow fall to the ground without God's knowledge? And "ye are of more value than many sparrows" (Matthew 10:31).

THE NATURE OF MANKIND

God is. Mankind exists (from the Latin, *ex,* out of, and *sistere,* to stand forth). *Humanity stands forth out of the universal Mind and Substance we call God.* As such, humanity is the fullest and most complete expression of God on the planet: "In the image and likeness of God, He created them" (Genesis. 1:27). To humanity, therefore, is given dominion over all other manifestations of life.

Jesus said, "one is your Father, He who is in heaven" (Matthew 23:9). He also said "ye are all brethren" (Matthew 23:8), because all of us are manifestations of one and the same Spirit.

As soon as we recognize this truth of our relationship to all humanity, we at once slip out of our narrow personal loves--out of "me" and "mine" into universal love, taking in all the world. Then, with Jesus, we joyfully exclaim: "'Who is my mother? And who are my brethren?' And behold he stretched forth his hand toward his disciples and said, behold my mother and my brethren" (Matthew 12:48).

HUMANITY'S RELATION WITH GOD

Each of us is a threefold being, made up of Spirit, body, and soul. Spirit, our innermost, real being, is the absolute part of us, the *I* of us, and has never changed—though our thoughts and circumstances may have changed thousands of times. This part of us is God standing forth into visibility. It's what Jesus called "the Father" in us. At this central core of our being, each of us can say, as Jesus did, "I and the Father are one" (John 10:30) and be speaking absolute truth.

God is the name we give to that unchanging principle that is the source of all existence. To the individual, God takes on personality as loving Father-Mother, a comforting Presence. But as the creative underlying cause of all things, God is principle, impersonal, infinite.

For some, taught to think of God as a person, the statement that God is Principle is chilling. Terrified, they cry out, "They have taken away my Lord, and I know not where they have laid him!" (John 20:13). But broader and wiser minds find the thought of God as a person too small for their understanding, for a person is limited in place and time, and God is the infinite within which the finite universe takes form.

All that we can ever need or desire is available to us through the infinite reservoir of good that we call God and that we experience as the loving Father-Mother Presence. We all have direct access through the central "I" of our being, the Spirit within, to the infinite life, love, wisdom and power that we call God. This Source is the living fountain of all good, the Giver of all good gifts. This Source and you are connected, every moment of your existence. You can draw on this Source for all the good that you are, or ever will be, capable of desiring. There is no limit to God's willingness to manifest more of God's self through us, when we are willing to align our self with God.

Until now in our lives, we've focused on the world outside of us to satisfy our desires—and we've been sorely disappointed. *Our hunger for satisfaction is not for physical experience; it's really the cry of the homesick child-soul for the Father-Mother God.* It's the Spirit's desire in us to experience—come into our consciousness as—more and more perfection, until we become fully aware of our oneness with All-perfection. Humanity has never been and never could be really satisfied with anything less.

What we want to know now is how to receive more from the fountainhead within, and how to experience more of the goodness that is God in our daily lives.

SUMMARY

- All things are one and the same Spirit manifesting in different ways;

- the reality standing under everything is the substance of God;

- all the various forms of life are one Life coming out in different forms;

- all the intelligence and wisdom of the world are God as Mind manifesting in different ways;

- all the love people feel and express toward each other is a "drop" of God as love made visible in human action.

LESSON THREE: THINKING

The Spirit within you *is* Divine Mind, the real mind. Without it, the human mind would disappear, just as a shadow disappears when the object that cast it is removed. With it, each of us has direct access to all there is in God—if we can be "as little children" and try a few, plain, simple rules that Jesus taught. By following them, we can find the Divine Mind within ourselves and can work out our salvation from all that troubles us.

UNDERSTANDING MIND

When we say that there is only one Mind in all the universe, and that this Mind is God, some people will see the connection with Lesson Two immediately.

Others will say, "If all the mind there is, is God, then how can I think wrong thoughts, or have any other than God thoughts?" The connection between universal Mind and our own individual minds is difficult, but can be understood.

There is in reality only one Mind: Spirit, which is life, intelligence, power, etc. in and through the universe. Yet human beings are, in a sense, individuals with free wills, and not puppets.

We are made up of three aspects: Spirit, soul, and body. Spirit is the unchanging "I" of us, the part that has never changed and, through all eternity, never will change. Soul is the clothing, if you will, of the Spirit, and body the clothing of the soul. Spirit is inner—one with God, unchanging. Mind, the intellect, is constantly changing and evolving, gathering its information from the world around, through the five senses, feeding the soul with its input.

Humanity, which lived originally as consciousness of the Spirit, has become more and more attached to the material, sensual aspect of the self, so our souls now include two minds: "the mind of the flesh" and "the mind of the Spirit." Paul told the Romans that "the mind of the flesh is death [sorrow, trouble, sickness], but the mind of the Spirit is life and peace" (Romans 8:6).

"Have this mind in you which was also in Christ Jesus," he told his students in Philippi (Philippians 2:5). He spoke of the Divine Mind of Spirit, which makes no mistakes.

FREE WILL

It may be difficult for some to understand why, if God lives in us all the time, we can be ignorant of and drift into these useless thoughts and the troubles that go with them. The answer is, simply, that we are not automatons. Your child would never learn to walk if you always did her walking. Because you realize that the only way for a child to be strong and self-reliant in all things is to let her try things on her own, you let her try and fail. You aren't willing to make a puppet out of your child by taking all the steps, even though you know she'll fall down many times, learning how.

We, too, are in the process of growing up. We're developing into the highest of spiritual beings. We get many falls and bumps along the way, but it's only through the process that our growth can proceed. Father and mother, no matter how deep their love for their children, can't grow for them—nor can God, who is Omnipotence at the center of our beings, grow for us spiritually without making us automatons instead of individuals.

EXPERIENCING TRUTH

If you want to make rapid progress in spiritual understanding, stop reading so many books. They only give you someone's opinion about Truth, or a sort of history of that author's seeking Truth. What you want is a revelation of Truth, the thoughts of God, in your own soul—and that will never come through reading books.

Seek light from the Spirit of truth within you. Go alone. Think alone. Seek light alone, and if it doesn't come at once, don't be discouraged and run off to someone else to get the light! You'll only get someone's opinion, and may then be further away from the Truth you're seeking than every before.

Someone has said that the smallest child, who has learned from the depths of her being to say "Our Father," is infinitely greater than the great intellect who has not yet learned it. The apostle Paul was considered such an intellect, a Pharisee among

Pharisees, but after he was enlightened by the Spirit, he said "the foolishness of God is wiser than men" (I Corinthians 1:25).

The Spirit of Truth is at your "beck and call." Seek it.

Shut down the intellect for the time being, and let the Universal Mind speak to you. Wait patiently for it to "guide you into all the truth" of all things, as we are told in the gospel of John (16:13). And when it speaks, though it may be only "a still, small voice" (as it was for the prophet in I Kings 19:12), you will know that what it says is Truth.

How will you know? You'll know just as you know you're alive. All the argument in the world to convince you against Truth that comes to you as direct revelation will fall flat and harmless at your side.

And the Truth that you *know*, not simply believe, you can use to help others. That which comes forth through Spirit in you will reach the soul of those to whom you speak. By contrast, what comes in from the outside, from the senses or intellect, reaches only the intellect of those you wish to serve. And the intellect loves to argue.

Intellect argues; Spirit reveals. One *may* be true; the other is *always* true. Spirit does not give opinions about Truth; it is Truth, and it reveals Itself.

THE POWER OF THOUGHT

What we think about God, about ourselves, and about others, makes a great difference in our daily lives. Till now, not understanding who we really are or the results of our thinking, we've let our thoughts flow in a random "stream of consciousness." Our minds have been turned outwardly and we've taken almost all information in through our senses. Because of that, we have thought incorrectly, and *all of our troubles and sorrows are the result of that incorrect thought process.*

"But wait," says someone, "I can't see how my thinking incorrect thoughts about God, or about anyone else, can make me sick or cause me to lose my job." Well, we won't try just now to explain all the steps by which undesirable results follow from incorrect thinking; for now, just try thinking true thoughts awhile, and see what happens.

Take the thought "God loves me." Think these words over and over continually for a few days, trying to realize that they are true, and see what the effects are on your body and situation.

For most people, something like the following happens. First, you get a new enthusiasm; then quicker, better circulation, with a pleasantly warm sensation, followed by better digestion. Later, as Truth flows out through your being into your surroundings, everybody will show more love for you without your knowing why; and finally, circumstances around you will begin to change, coming into harmony with your desires, instead of against them.

Everyone has heard how intense thoughts of grief or fear have turned peoples' hair white in a few hours. We've all experienced how fear makes the heart beat so rapidly as to seem about to "jump out of the body"—even if we only imagined it! In the same way, intense negative thoughts can cause painful disease.[12] Carrying emotional burdens makes more stooped shoulders than carrying heavy physical loads. Believing that God regards us as "miserable sinners" and is constantly watching our activities with disapproval, discourages and half-paralyzes some people, leading to failure in all they try.

FOCUSING THOUGHT

If you keep your thoughts turned toward the external of yourself, or of others, you will see only the things that are not real, that pass away. All the faults, the failures, or the lacks in people or circumstances will seem very real to you, and you will be unhappy or sick.

By contrast, if you turn your thoughts away from outer appearances and toward the spiritual, dwelling on the good in yourself and others, all the apparent evil will first drop out of your thought and then out of your life. This is what Paul was saying in his letter to the members of the church at Philippi:

---

[12] Many recent studies in the field of psychoneuroimmunology have linked illnesses ranging from ulcers to arthritis to cancer to the patient's habitual thought patterns.

Finally, brethren, whatsoever things are true, whatsoever things are honorable, whatsoever things are just, whatsoever things are pure, whatsoever things are lovely, whatsoever things are of good repute, if there be any virtue and if there be any praise, think on these things (Philippians 4:8).

RADIATING FOUNTAINS

We can all learn how to turn our awareness, or conscious mind, to the universal Mind, or Spirit, within us. We can, through practice, learn how to make this every-day, topsy-turvy "mind of the flesh" be still, and let the Mind that we call God (all-wisdom, all-love) think in us and through us.

Imagine, if you will, a huge reservoir, out of which lead many small streams and rivulets. At the far end, each stream opens out into a small fountain. Each one of these fountains is continually filled and replenished from the reservoir, and it is giving out in all directions the water that flows through it, so that all who come are refreshed and blessed.

This is our relation to God: each of us, no matter how small or ignorant, is a little fountain at the end of the stream, receiving God from the reservoir and radiating it out in all directions.

The fountain represents our individuality, apparently separate from God, the reservoir. Still, the fountain is one with God in that we are constantly renewed and fed from the reservoir, without which we are nothing. Each of us, no matter how insignificant we are in the world, may receive unlimited good through the fountain at our center, and radiate it out to all. And, radiate it we must, if we are to receive more. Stagnation is death.

ONLY WE BLOCK THE FLOW

The very wisdom of God—the love, the life, and the power of God—are ready and waiting with longing impulse to flow out through us without limit! When it flows through the intellect of some people, everyone says, "what a wonderful mind!" When it flows through the hearts of others, we see love that melts all bitterness, envy, selfishness, and jealousy before it. When it flows through a body, as life, no disease can compete with it.

We don't have to beg and plead and bargain with God, any more than we must beg the sun to shine! The sun shines because it's the law of its being to shine, and it can't help it. No more can God help pouring unto us unlimited wisdom, life, power—all good—because *it is the law of God's being to do so.*

Nothing can hinder God's flowing except our own lack of understanding. The sun may shine ever so brightly, but if we have, through willfulness or ignorance, placed ourselves (or been placed by our ancestors) in the deepest corner of a dark cellar, we get neither joy nor comfort from its shining; to those in the cellar, the sun never shines.

So, up to now, we haven't known how to get ourselves out of the cellar of ignorance, doubt, and despair. To most of us, therefore, it's seemed that God has held back from us the life, wisdom, power that we wanted so much. All our searching seemed in vain.

But the sun doesn't radiate life and warmth one day and darkness and chill the next. Nor does God radiate love at one time and anger or displeasure at another. As the head of the Jerusalem church after Jesus' ascension said, "Does the fountain send forth from the same opening sweet water and bitter? Can a fig tree, my brethren, yield olives, or a vine figs?" (James 3:11).

SUMMARY

- There is but one Mind in the universe.

- Human mind, the intellect, makes mistakes because it gathers its information from the outside world through the senses.

- Universal Mind sees and speaks from within; it is all Truth.

- Our ways of thinking make our happiness or unhappiness, our success or lack of success, and we can, with effort, change our ways of thinking.

- God is at all times, regardless of our action or inaction, trying to pour more good into our lives to make them richer, fuller, and more successful.

LESSON FOUR: DENYING THE POWER OF ILLUSIONS

Every religion through all the ages has had some sort of denial as one of its foundations. The idea of denial has been so powerful that devout seekers have even tortured their bodies in various ways, believing that they were making themselves more spiritual, or at least were placating some angry god.

These are misunderstandings of God's intention for us, and among Christians, they come from a misinterpretation of the gospel verse:

> Then Jesus said to his disciples, if any man will come after me, let him deny himself and take up his cross and follow me (Matthew 16:24).

Many people think this means that if anyone wants to please God they must give up all their enjoyment and comfort, all the things they like and want, and take up the heavy cross of constantly doing things that they'd rather not (which is why so many young people have put off "being Christian" until they're "old!").

There could be nothing further from Jesus' meaning than this.

FALSE BELIEFS AND THEIR CONSEQUENCES

In our ignorance of God's true nature, we've believed that all our enjoyment must come from external sources—usually from something we don't yet have. The poor see enjoyment only in having lots of money. The rich, often experiencing "too much of a good thing," complain that life holds no happiness. The sick are convinced that if they were well, they would be happy. The healthy but hard working person seeks rest and recreation for enjoyment. And so forth.

Our intellect tends to seek changes in our outward conditions to achieve enjoyment. So we move, take new jobs, try new relationships, and so on. Then, in old age, when people have tried everything, acquiring all kinds of things to fill the emptiness, and have too often been sadly disappointed, then they turn to God. And, believing God to be far off in some other place, they try to find some comfort in the belief that sometime, somewhere, they'll get what they want and be happy. They become patient and submissive, but never truly happy.

But having more of God doesn't take the good things out of our lives, or even delay it; it only puts more of them in, now. Everyone desires to have only good in their lives and surroundings. We all want to live lives full of love, to be perfectly healthy, to know all interesting and needful things, to have great power and much joy—and this is exactly what our loving Father wants for us. All good, of whatever kind, is God made visible. When we are craving any good thing, we're really craving more of God to come forth in our lives so we can experience it with our senses.

Jesus, the master teacher of Truth, understood this. He spent nearly three years teaching common, everyday people like us, who wanted the same things we do: food and the rent and clothing, money, friends, and love. He taught them to love their enemies and do good to those who persecuted them, to avoid resisting evil but to give *double* to anyone who tried to taken anything away from them, and to stop worrying about things like clothing or shelter because "your heavenly Father knows that you need those things" (Matthew 2:32).

Then one day Jesus said, "I've told you these things so my joy might remain in you and your joy might be full" (John 15:11). And He said, "Whatever you ask of the Father in my name, it shall be done..." (John 15:16). These don't sound like the words of someone who believed we were intended to go without the comforts of life—or in any way deprive or torture ourselves!

MISTAKEN BELIEFS

As we learned in Lesson Three, however, there is a "carnal" or "fleshly" mind in each of us that, because it works from the senses and intellect, is not to be relied on completely. *This* is the self of which Jesus spoke when He said "let him deny himself." This intellect, this "carnal mind," this ego, or whatever you wish to call it, is envious and jealous, fearful, fretful, and sick, because it is selfish. This "small self," or "Adam self" seeks its own gratification at any cost—even causing its own death to prove itself right. We have believed all that this mind has told us; we've accepted its false beliefs about ourselves and God; and so we've experienced suffering and lack.

Our real, "sacred" self is never sick, never afraid, never selfish. It's the part of us that Paul called *caritas,* meaning "heart-center" and usually translated as "love or charity," which, he says, "seeks not her own, is not easily provoked, and thinks no evil" (I Corinthians 13:5). Our real self is always seeking to share and serve others, while the "small self," frightened by its own beliefs and fantasies, seeks to own and control.

We have been believing falsehoods. We have believed that God was human-like, distant from us, and angry with us, and that we were "sinners" who ought to be afraid of Him. We have believed that pain and sickness and poverty and other troubles are evil things put here by this same God to torture us in some way into loving and serving Him. We've believed that we pleased God most when we were subdued by our troubles and became patiently submissive—not even trying to overcome them.

All this is false! Entirely false! And *the first step toward freeing ourselves from sickness, pain, sorrow—all our troubles—is to get rid of these erroneous beliefs about God and about ourselves.*

Some may doubt that wrong belief can affect our bodies or our situation. If so, consider the child who is so afraid of the "monster" under the bed that he has convulsions. Or imagine if you received a message that someone you love who is absent from you, has been severely injured or even killed—your emotional, physical, and perhaps even financial suffering would be just as great, even if the message were proven false some weeks later. In the same way, our imaginary "monsters" of divine wrath, and false messages declaring death and destruction, affect our bodies and emotions. [13]

---

[13] America's first metaphysical healer, Phineas P. Quimby, blamed preachers and doctors for instilling in people the beliefs that caused their illness—and achieved much of his success by simply showing his patients how erroneous those beliefs were.

Changing Our Beliefs

There are people who've learned how to change beliefs, and so change the conditions of their life. One of the methods they've found gets rid of disturbing conditions every time: denying the power and existence of those conditions, absolutely. First we deny that any outward circumstances have any power to make us unhappy. Second, we deny that any conditions other than God's omnipresent good could exist at all.

According to Webster, the word "deny" has two definitions. In one sense, to deny is to withhold from, as to deny bread to the hungry. In another sense (which is most likely how Jesus used it), to deny is to declare to be not true, to repudiate as utterly false.

To "deny oneself," then, is not to withhold comfort or happiness, but to *deny the reality of* one's human, or "small" self. It is to deny the validity of the claims and beliefs the "small self" holds on to so determinedly.

If you've done something incorrectly, the first step toward getting it right is to undo what's been done wrong and begin again from that point. Denial is the first practical step toward wiping out of our minds the mistaken beliefs of a lifetime. We declare not to be true that which appears to be true but is based on mistaken beliefs. Jesus taught, "Judge not by appearances..." (John 7:24). And *all negative appearances are directly opposed to Truth.*

For example, it appears that the sun moves around the earth, rising in the east and setting in the west. If you believed that to be true and someone demonstrated to you that the appearance is not the truth, then the only way you could undo the old belief is to consistently deny the reality of the appearance—even as the evidence of the senses says otherwise.

Similarly, it appears that our bodies and circumstances control our thoughts—but the opposite is true: our thoughts control our bodies and our circumstances. This means that we must repeatedly deny the idea that anyone or anything outside of us can affect our mood or our wellbeing if we are to let go of the appearance in favor of Truth. *If you repeatedly deny a false or disturbing appearance, it loses its power to disturb.*

People who have grown out of trouble and sickness through daily practice have found it useful to cleanse themselves of the distressing effects of having believed ideas that they were separate from God. So, we may see the possibility of our inheritance, of our own Spirit-being which never changes, but if we are to realize this Truth, we need to realize our oneness with the Creator at all times. And in order to realize it, we must deny, in ourselves and others, any appearances that seem contrary to this. We deny their reality. We declare that they are not true.

COMMON BELIEFS TO BE DENIED

Four common beliefs, granted power by most people, and affecting them in myriad ways, can be denied like this:

1. There is no evil in omnipresent good.

2. There is no absence of life, substance, or intelligence, anywhere.

3. Pain, sickness, poverty, old age, and death are illusions and cannot affect me.

4. There is nothing at all in the universe for me to fear.

There is no evil. There is only one power in the universe, and that is God: good. So apparent evils are nothing in themselves. They can have no power; they're simply the appearance of the absence of good, just as darkness is the apparent absence of light.[14] But good, as God, is omnipresent, so the apparent absence of good must be an illusion, like the appearance of the sun "moving" across the sky.

There is no absence of substance, life, intelligence, anywhere. Everything that exists stands forth from God: is the Substance of God, the good. Therefore, God as Substance, Life, Wisdom and Intelli-

---

[14] Much of what we call "darkness" is filled with light that is either too fast or too slow for us to see. For example, infra-red scopes help us to see objects that we would otherwise miss with our normal vision.

gence is omnipresent—everywhere present—and none of these qualities can be absent, anywhere.[15]

Pain, sickness, poverty, old age, and death are illusions and cannot affect me. God is eternal life. God lives in and through each of us and is the "I" of you, the truth of you. The "I" that you truly are, therefore, knows only eternal wellbeing and can never be touched by material illusions. Paul reminded the church at Corinth that "the things which are seen are temporal, but the things which are not seen are eternal" (II Corinthians 4:18).

There is nothing in all the universe for me to fear. God's presence in us, as the "I" of us, is omnipotent—all power—so there can be no power greater than the "I" that you are. More, God's omnipresence as good means that All That Is is good—and there can be no thing, anywhere, to cause us to fear. The universe is, as Einstein hoped to prove, "a friendly place."

You need not wait to understand fully the implications of these denials—nor even why you deny them. Simply begin to practice denying these mistaken beliefs in an unprejudiced way and see how wonderfully they will, after a while, deliver you from some of the so-called "evils" of modern life.

Repeat these four denials silently several times a day—not with effort or anxiety, but calmly realizing the meaning of the words spoken. Speak them silently or aloud, but not in a way to create antagonism or invite discussion.

1. There is no evil in omnipresent good.
2. There is no absence of life, substance, or intelligence, anywhere.
3. Pain, sickness, poverty, old age, and death are illusions and cannot affect me.
4. There is nothing at all in the universe for me to fear.

DENYING DISTRESS

Denial of distressing or disturbing experiences brings freedom from bondage to the world around us, and happiness comes

---

[15] Cady's teacher, Emma Hopkins, used to say "There, where the idiot stands, is infinite wisdom and intelligence fully present!"

when we can effectively deny the power of anything to touch or trouble us.

Almost hourly for most people, little issues and fears come up in life. Meet each one with a denial. Calmly and coolly say to yourself, "That's nothing at all; it can't hurt me nor make me unhappy." Don't fight against the issue. Let your denial be the denial of any possible superiority over you, even effect on you, just as you would deny the power of ants in their hill disturbing you where you stand across the road.

If you feel anger, stand still and silently deny its power. Say that you are not subject to anger; you are Spirit, love made manifest, and cannot be made angry—and the anger will leave you.

If someone seems to be mean or appears to try to hurt you, remember that God's substance and Spirit are alive in you and silently deny the possibility that anyone would act in such a way.

If you feel jealousy, envy, any form of distress, deny the power of such emotions over you. Declare that you are really Spirit, love made manifest, and that such feelings cannot exist as part of you. Declare further the truth that all people are one and the same Spirit. Shall the foot be jealous of the hand, or the ear envy the eye? Remember that in reality you, however insignificant you may be in the world's eyes, are absolutely necessary for God to be the perfect wholeness that Is.

If you find yourself dreading to meet someone or afraid to step out and do what you want or have promised to do, immediately begin to deny the power of fear. Say, "It's not true. I am Spirit, and no one—nothing— exists in the universe to harm me; I have nothing to fear." Soon you'll find that all the fear has disappeared; all the anxiety is gone.

To some, this mechanical approach may seem a strange way into a more spiritual life. But our thoughts determine our experience and changing our thoughts is an essential first step toward experiencing Spirit in and around us, every moment of every day. Practicing these steps wholeheartedly and without prejudice is the very best thing we can do for growth in divine knowledge and fullness of joy in everything we undertake.

CREATING OUR CIRCUMSTANCES

Chances are you've been living in negative thinking for years, denying your ability to succeed, denying your good health, denying your Godhood, denying your power to accomplish many things. That pattern of denials has paralyzed you and weakened your power in the world.

When, in the next lesson, you learn the opposite of denial—the use of affirmations—you'll discover how to lift yourself out of the realm of distress into the realm of success.

For now, remember: *no person or thing in the universe, no chain of circumstances, can come between you and all joy, all good.* You may think something stands between you and your heart's desire, and so live with that desire unfulfilled, but it's simply not true. This "think" is the bugaboo under the bed that has no reality. Deny its reality. Deny it and you'll realize that this appearance was false. Deny it and you will find yourself free. Then you'll see the good flowing toward you and into you, and you will understand clearly that *nothing can come between you and your own.*

This is your work, and its results will be felt around you when you have fully realized the truth of the words you speak.

SUMMARY

- Having more God in our lives doesn't take away the good things, it puts in more, now.

- Our mistaken beliefs about God and ourselves cause all our suffering, loss, and distress.

- There is no evil in omnipresent good.

- There is no absence of life, substance, or intelligence, anywhere.

- Pain, sickness, poverty, old age, and death are illusions and cannot affect us.

- There is no one and nothing at all in the universe for us to fear.

- As Spirit, disturbing emotions are not part of us and have no power over us.

LESSON FIVE: AFFIRMATIONS, TOOLS FOR LIVING

Most people start out on a spiritual journey because they're dissatisfied with their present life. The human mind is convinced that somewhere, somehow, it ought to be able to bring to itself whatever it desires and would satisfy it. This thought is simply a shadow of the reality.

The hunger we feel is the prompting of the Spirit within us, which longs with an infinite longing to fill us. It's one side of the spiritual law of supply and demand, with the other side being unchangeably and unfailingly the promise: "All things whatever that you pray and ask for, believe that you receive them and you shall have them" (Mark 11:24).

We can all reach a state where we can stop our doing because we realize that Spirit is the fulfillment of all our desires. We simply become still and know that all the things we desire are ours already. This knowing, or recognition, has the power to bring the invisible Good—the innermost Substance of things—into precisely the visible form we have desired.

But to get to that state we must take the first steps faithfully, earnestly, and trustingly, even though it may seem at first glance as useless and empty as the ancient rituals and ceremonies of the high church have seemed.

THE NATURE OF AFFIRMATIONS

Those who have carefully studied spiritual laws find that, besides being freed from apparent evil by denying its reality of power, they can also bring any desired good into their lives by persistently claiming that it's already here.

We call these claims Affirmations. And to affirm anything is to assert positively that it is so—even in the face of evidence to the contrary.

We may not be able to see how, by our simply affirming a thing to be true, that we can make it happen—especially a thing that to all human reasoning or sight doesn't seem true at all. We can, however, compel our minds to stop arguing and go to work to prove the rule.

Spiritual laws can't always be expressed verbally, but they are nonetheless infallible and immutable laws that work with precision and certainty. The beautiful Presence within us and around us is the substance of every good we could possibly desire—even more than we can desire, for "eye has not seen, nor ear heard, neither have entered the heart of man, the things God has prepared for them that love…" (I Corinthians 2:9).

USING AFFIRMATIONS

In some way, difficult to say in words, there's power in our word of faith that brings all good things directly into our daily life.

We speak the word. We confidently affirm. But we have nothing to do with bringing it to pass.

Job was told, after he reconciled with God, "You also shall decree a thing and it shall be established unto you" (Job 22:28). So we decree, or affirm, unwaveringly and steadfastly. We hold God by His own unchanging laws to do the establishing or fulfilling.

Saying over and over any affirmation or denial is a re-training of a mind that has been so long affirming and denying based on mistaken beliefs that it needs this constant repetition of the Truth to function in alignment with it.

You do not change God's attitude one little bit by either begging or affirming. You only change your attitude toward God. By saying these words you put yourself in alignment with divine law, which is always working for your good (and never toward harm or punishment!). Your real self, the "I" of you, knows this and lives this, always.

GENERAL AFFIRMATIONS

As with the denials, so with the affirmations. There are a few sweeping affirmations of Truth that cover many smaller ones, and which are wonderfully effective in bringing good to our own experience and to others.

1. God is life, love, intelligence, substance, omnipotence, omniscience, omnipresence.

2. God's life, love, wisdom and power flow into and through all that is, including me, in every moment; I am a manifestation of God's omnipresent substance, one with God and governed by divine law.

3. I am Spirit: perfect, holy, harmonious; nothing can hurt me or make me sick or afraid, for Spirit cannot be hurt or sick or afraid; I manifest my real self through this body now.

4. God works in me to will and do whatever is my fulfillment, and God cannot fail.

First, *God is Life, Love, Intelligence, Substance, Omnipotence, Omniscience, Omnipresence.* These are ideas we learned in the second lesson. As you repeat them, please remember that every particle of life, love, intelligence, power, or real substance in the universe is simply a degree of God made manifest in form. Try to think of what it means. God is omnipresent, everywhere present, and God is good. Then why fear? God is omnipotent, all power, so what other power could prevail? You will soon realize that God is all form, everywhere. Then you will find yourself forever putting aside the idea of a devil, or evil, as an adverse power that might bring harm to someone—*there is and can be only one power, one presence, and that is God, the good.* Knowing this, you can stand true and unwavering if you are ever faced with the appearance of evil in any form. Doing so, you shall see the seeming evil melt away like the darkness before the light, and the good that was always there will become manifest.

Second, *God's life, love, wisdom and power flow into and through all that is, including me, in every moment; I am a manifestation of God's omnipresent substance, one with God and governed by divine law.* Remember while repeating this affirmation that nothing—no situation no person, no group of people—can in any way stand between you and the Source of your life, wisdom, or power. It is all to be found in the innermost Spirit of your being.

Nothing but your own ignorance of how to receive, or your own willfulness, can hinder your having unlimited supply. No matter how lacking you feel--how weak or sick or inefficient you've called yourself—take your eyes and thoughts off the appearance and turn them within to the central fountain there. And, as you do so, state calmly, quietly, with absolute assurance: *"This appearance is false; God, manifest as life, wisdom, power, is no flowing through my entire being and through me into the world around me."* You'll see a marvelous change in your self as a result of the realization that this spoken word brings to you.

Third, *I am Spirit: perfect, holy, harmonious; nothing can hurt me or make me sick or afraid, for Spirit cannot be hurt or sick or afraid; I manifest my real self through this body now.* Your real self, the "I" of you, understands this perfectly, but you have identified with the human, carnal mind instead of your Self. These words will help shift that identification and allow you to experience your birthright.

Fourth, *God works in me to will and do whatever is my fulfillment, and God cannot fail.* Our affirming God's mind working both to will and to do makes us will only the good. And since God, the Father in us, does the works, there can be no failure of action or thought. Whatsoever we fully commit to the Father within to do, and affirm is done, we shall see accomplished.[16]

This set of affirmations, along with the denials given in Lesson Four, takes a major place in the first instructions given to students of Truth. For now, the student must memorize and repeat them often, Later, the students' own experience and inner guidance lead them to an understanding of divine law that makes it easier for them to follow Jesus' simple rules.

THE POWER OF THE CLAIM

Wonderfully, these affirmations and denials will act to deliver you out of the greatest external distresses—even places where no human help prevails. It's as though the moment we assert emphatically our oneness with God the Father, all the power of omnipotent love is instantly set into motion to rush to our rescue and

---

16 In her *How I Used Truth* Cady describes her own experience of the importance of claiming—after giving up charging for her services and nearly fainting from hunger for having forgotten to claim her supply.

support. And when you feel that power has begun to work for you, you can stop doing things, boldly claiming *"It is done; I have the desires of my heart."*

Those who have claimed their inheritance by calmly affirming their oneness with God, know how free they can be from human effort and planning. This power has healed the sick, brought joy in place of mourning, and literally opened prison doors, inviting the prisoner to go free—all without ever a request for human assistance.

In reality, God is always moving within us to manifest All-Good more fully through us. Our affirming, backed by our faith, is the link connecting conscious human needs and desires with God's power and supply. "You open your hand and satisfy the desires of every living thing," was David's joyful declaration of this law (Psalm 145:16).

GUIDELINES

It's important to understand that it's not necessarily these particular words that have done the job. Our denying apparent evil and, regardless of appearances, affirming good to be all there is and our oneness with God's omnipotent power to accomplish, even when there are not visible signs of God working, that has accomplished the feat. In one case, simply claiming, "God is your defense and deliverance!" opened all the doors to restore a man to his family in a month—after five years of efforts by lawyers to return him from exile.

No definite rules can be provided for what will be most effective. A few hints, however, may be helpful.

Some people get better results from repeating denials; others do better when they use more affirmations than denials. Denials tend to erase or dissolve. Affirmations build up and give strength or power.

Denials cleanse the mind and blot out of memory all seeming evil and unhappiness, so they feel more like a dream, so people who remember vividly and are inclined to dwell on past pains or sorrows need to repeat denials frequently. Denials are particularly effective for people who are intolerant, judgmental, or aggressively immoral, or those who have become overconfident in their human capacity. Denials are also important for those who have become addicted, for the selfish, and any who find it easy to lash out at others.

Affirmations are most powerful for those who feel inefficient or incompetent, those who are afraid of others or "give in" easily, and those who are anxious or doubtful. Affirmations help those in positions of responsibility, as well.

People who are self-negating or passive need to use more affirmations and people who are self-confident or unforgiving need more denials.

If there comes a time when you're confused about what to say or do, stand still and affirm, *"God in me is infinite wisdom; I always know just what to do."* Then act on whatever comes to mind in the stillness that follows. Don't worry, but depend fully on the principles and you'll be surprised at the sudden inspiration that comes to you. "For I will give you a mouth and wisdom, which all your adversaries will not be able to withstand or outdo" (Luke 21:15).

Deny the appearance of evil or harm; affirm good. Deny weakness; affirm strength. Deny any undesirable condition and affirm the good that you desire. The principle always works.

Practice these denials and affirmations silently while you walk, in the car, when you're awake at night—anywhere and everywhere. Soon you'll begin to experience a wonderful mastery over external things, and over yourself.

Denying and Affirming can be used to solve any of life's problems, regardless of the nature of the problem. This principle frees us, inheritors of the Kingdom, from all undesirable conditions. It's what Jesus meant when he said "believe that you receive them and you shall have them" (Mark 11:24). It always brings good into peoples' lives.

All we need do is use these simple rules and practice them faithfully, until they lead us into such complete realization of our own Godhood that we no longer need to depend on them.

SUMMARY

- We can bring any desired good into our lives by persistently claiming that it's already here.

- Denying and Affirming can be used to solve any of life's problems, regardless of the nature of the problem; denials tend to erase or dissolve; affirmations build up and give strength or power.

- God is life, love, intelligence, substance, omnipotence, omniscience, omnipresence.

- God's life, love, wisdom and power flow into and through all that is, including me, in every moment; I am a manifestation of God's omnipresent substance, one with God and governed by divine law.

- I am Spirit: perfect, holy, harmonious; nothing can hurt me or make me sick or afraid, for Spirit cannot be hurt or sick or afraid; I manifest my real self through this body now.

- God works in me to will and do whatever is my fulfillment, and God cannot fail.

LESSON SIX: FAITH, THE MASTER KEY

The word faith is typically thought to mean a simple form of belief based mostly on ignorance and superstition. It's been scorned by "thinking people"—those who've believed that intellectual attainment is the highest form of knowledge. "Blind faith," they disdainfully refer to it—fit only for the ignorant, children, and the clergy—not a practical thing to build a life on.

These people pride themselves in having outgrown their childish, blind, unreasoning faith. They say they've reached a more mature state—believing only the things they've seen or can logically explain based on what they've seen.

The apostle Paul was a Greek Jew trained as a Hebrew scholar, a Pharisee. And, as his many letters illustrate, he was obviously a highly intellectual man. In his letter to the Hebrew Christians (the original "Jews for Jesus") he defined faith as follows: "Faith is the substance of things hoped for, the evidence of things not seen" (Hebrews 11:1), having already explained that "… things which are seen were not made of things we can sense" (Heb 11:3). We can interpret this as meaning that our faith, as substance, brings into the world of evidence the things we hope for that were not seen.

This means that *whatever we desire is in the invisible substance surrounding us and takes form according to our faith.*

Paul goes on to describe the many instances in the Old Testament of things brought to pass, not by anyone's efforts, but by faith, reminding his audience of all those "who through faith subdued kingdoms, stopped the mouths of lions, quenched the power of fire, escaped the edge of the sword, were made strong, waxed mighty in war, turned to flight armies of aliens. Women received their dead by a resurrection …" (Hebrews 11:32). [17]

---

[17] While some will say that the Old Testament is a book of "fairy tales" rather than history, others are finding more and more evidence of events described therein. Still others are finding evidence in other cultures of similar events, suggesting that faith-based ac-

Do you want any more power than this? More than the power to subdue kingdoms, turn armies to flight, stop the mouths of lions, quench fire, and raise the dead to life again?

Even if you *do* want more than this, don't despair—or even hesitate to claim them—for One who knew what He was talking about said "All things are possible to him who believes" (Mark 9:23).

Most people raised on these ideas have felt, whenever anyone has spoken of faith "as to move mountains," a sort of hopeless despair. Even if we believed God holds all good things in His hand and is willing to dole them out according to our faith, we've wondered, how could we hope to please Him? We've questioned our ability to reach a high enough level of faith. We've wondered whether, in fact, there is such power, when we've not seen it in our lives before. We're like the disciples following Jesus, to whom he said, "Oh ye of little faith!"

As a result, it's no wonder that logical minds have considered faith a wispy thing, good enough for the weak to hang their hopes on but not something from which real, definite results could ever be obtained.

BLIND FAITH & UNDERSTANDING FAITH

There is, indeed, blind faith. It's the instinctive trust in a power greater than ourselves. Some have said that it's better than no faith, for it will open its eyes in time. It is, for many, the first step toward a full life.

But there is also an understanding faith. Understanding faith is built on a realization of unchanging principle. Its action is intellectually understood, but goes far beyond intellectual conclusions. Faith goes beyond the intellect because it doesn't depend on physical facts, nor on the evidence of the senses—both of which are limited, temporary. Faith is born of the eternal Spirit of Truth at the center of our being. We call the Voice of that Spirit, intuition.

---

complishments may be far more prevalent across humanity than many intellectuals would have us believe.

Intuition is the open end, within our own being, of the invisible stream connecting us with that infinite reservoir of substance and wisdom that we call God. Faith is a ray of light shot out from the central sun, God, and enters our being through the open window of intuition.

With "blind" faith, we perceive the ray of light and, though intellect may not comprehend, we feel it opening out to all there is of God. We call this faith "blind" because, though it's based on Truth, we're not aware of it at the time.

Understanding faith knows positively the nature of the laws under which we're operating. They're like the laws of geometry. For example, the sum of the angles of a triangle always equals the sum of two right angles. No matter how large or small the triangle, nor where it's located, this law always holds. It's certain. And even before the triangle is actually drawn we know that it will be so. They're like the laws of arithmetic: the sum of the integers 1 plus 1 will always equal 2.[18] And whether we believe it or not, we will always get the same result.

The laws of Spirit and Mind are just as real and unchanging as the laws that govern mathematics—and even more consistent than the laws of matter, which change with scale, from very small (quantum mechanics) to "classical" (apples, baseballs, and rockets), to astronomical.

In Spiritual law there is no change with scale or focus: *if we have certain conditions of the mind, we must have certain results in our experience.* And this doesn't happen because we believe some wise person's testimony, nor even because our intuition tells us it is so, but because it is based on a law that can neither fail nor be broken.

---

[18] Some may remember the old joke in which an accountant, when asked what 1+1 equals, replied "what do you want it to?" Or they may recall adding the rational numbers 1.4 +1.4, each of which is rounded to 1, and getting the result 2.8, which is rounded to 3. The integers, however, being whole numbers, will always equal 2.

THE SPIRITUAL LAW OF SUPPLY & DEMAND

One of the unerring truths of our universe (spiritual and material) is that there's already abundance to supply every human desire: *there's a supply of good for every demand.*

The creative cause of all things is Spirit. Spirit, as the substance, the real essence of all that is, includes the sum total of all good. There is no good that you can desire in your life that is not Spiritual substance, and this Substance is all around us waiting to come forth into manifestation. Spirit, or God, is unlimited; therefore this good Substance all around us is unlimited, and is the supply of every need that exists in the visible, material world.

Another truth is that *the demand must be made before the good can come forth to fulfill it.*

What most people call the promises of God are certain, eternal truths that are true whether we read them in the Bible or the almanac. They are unvarying statements that cannot be changed. According to Webster, a promise is something sent beforehand to indicate that something unseen is on the way. It's a declaration, giving the person who receives it the right to expect and claim the performance.

When Jesus said, "Ask and you shall receive" (John 16:24), He was simply stating an absolute truth. He knew that the instant we desire, or express our desire by asking, we touch an infinite stream that starts on its way toward us the good we are seeking. He knew there need be no begging or pleading about it; that our asking is simply complying with an unfailing law that *must* work— there is no escape from it. Asking and receiving are two ends of the same thing, just as are 2 ones and a 2.

HEART'S DESIRE/GOD'S DESIRE

What is desire? *Our heart's desire is always God tapping at the door of our consciousness with infinite supply*—a supply that is useless without a demand for it.

The prophet Isaiah heard, "Before they call, I will answer" (Isa. 65:24). Before you're even aware of any lack or desire for more happiness or fullness of delight, the great Father-Mother Spirit dwelling in your heart has desired them for you. When you feel a desire emerging, you're feeling God in you desiring—even though you think it's only you, separate from God, wishing. Someone has said, "desire for anything is the thing itself, incipient." In other words, the thing coming toward you is what has sparked the desire!

There is, right now, an unlimited supply of all good, held in the unseen for every human being. In spite of any evidence to the contrary, *no one must have less so another may have more.* Your very own good is waiting for you, and your understanding faith is the power that brings it to you.

God lets us know about the infinite supply available to us by gently pushing on the divine "I" at the core of our being. God wants you to be a strong, self-sufficient man or woman, to have more power and dominion over the world around you. So, quietly, gently, God pushes a little more readiness, in the form of desire, into the center of your being. God extends into and expands your real Self, and you become aware of a desire to be more: more capable, stronger, with more impact on the world. Without Spirit expanding at the center of your being, you would never think of new desires, would simply remain content as you were.

When you think you want better health, more love, a brighter, more cheerful home all your very own, what you really want is more good in your life. And this is God pushing at the inner door of your being, as if saying "My dear child, let me in so I can give you all good and you can be happy."

Remember this: *desire in the heart for anything is God's sure promise sent beforehand that it's yours already in the realm of supply, and you can have it whenever you're ready.*

Accept the gift. Take it. You're merely fulfilling the Law of Supply and Demand. As Elijah did when he affirmed rain when not a small cloud was visible, affirm that you have the good you desire. Have faith in it. You are working with Spirit and you cannot fail. Let no one talk you out of it—"All things whatever you pray and ask for, believe that you receive them and you shall have them" (Mark 11:24).

43

FULFILLING DESIRES

We know the law of abundant supply, and the truth that supply always precedes the demand (demand being the call that makes the supply visible). We know that all desire in the heart for any good is really God's desire in us and for us. Now the question becomes: how shall we obtain the fulfillment of those desires, quickly and effortlessly?

It's simple, really, "Delight yourself also in the Creator Spirit and he will give you the desires of your heart (Psalm 37:4). Look into your heart and rejoice in God's working in and around you. Thank God that you *have*—not "will have" but *have now*—the desires of your heart, always. It helps to remember that the desire is the thing itself, letting us know it's ready to become manifest.

Truly, if the good you desire were not already yours, you could never, by any means, desire it. And if you're not sure you accept this idea, think of all the good things in the world you *don't* want, and couldn't imagine yourself desiring.

Some might ask, "What if I desire my neighbor's wife or property?"

You do not and cannot desire that which belongs to another!

You want its qualities in equivalent form; what your neighbor's possession stands for in your mind. If you think you desire your neighbor's spouse, what you really desire is the love that is represented there. Accept that you desire to fill your heart's craving for love. Affirm that *there is a rightful and overflowing supply of love for you*, and claim its manifestation in your life, now. It will appear as soon as you have released your blocks against it, and your desire to possess someone else's spouse will disappear.

Emerson, in his essay on *Compensation*, said that the man who knows this law "is sure that his welfare is dear to the heart of Being ... he cannot escape from his good." Knowing divine law and acting according to it, we can rest forever from all anxiety about the future, all fear of lack or want.

SUMMARY

- Whatever we desire is in the invisible substance surrounding us and takes form according to our faith.

- Blind faith is the instinctive trust in a power greater than ourselves.

- Understanding faith is built on a realization of unchanging principle; it's born of the eternal Spirit of Truth at the center of our being, the voice of which is called intuition.

- In Spiritual law, if we have certain conditions of the mind, we must have certain results in our experience.

- There's already abundance enough to supply every human desire.

- If the good you desire were not already yours, you could never, by any means, desire it—you do not and cannot desire anything that does not already exist or that belongs to another.

- We obtain the fulfillment of our desires quickly and effortlessly when we rejoice in God's working in and around us; we thank God that we *have*—not "will have" but *have now*—the desires of our hearts, always.

LESSON SEVEN: PERSONALITY & INDIVIDUALITY

One of the greatest beauties of the Sermon on the Mount is the simplicity of its language. Jesus the Nazarene always spoke simply, often in stories that even a child could understand. Yet he was the fullest, most complete manifestation of the One Mind that we know. More of the Wisdom that is God came forth through Him into visibility than through anyone else.

In fact, the more anyone manifests true Wisdom, the simpler are their ways of thinking and acting; the simpler, also, are the words they use to express their ideas. In his essay, *Oversoul*, Emerson said, "Converse with a mind that is grandly simple and all literature looks like word-catching."

Most metaphysical literature is anything but simple. Most of it is very confusing for those who haven't taken a series of courses on the subject. Two words, in particular, are often confusing in their usage: ego and Self.

DEFINING TERMS

Ego is the Latin word for "I." Sigmund Freud used the word to distinguish between that part of our minds which we're aware of (ego) from those which we don't usually identify with or observe. These others he called the "id," from the Latin for "thing," referring to the body-oriented subconscious mind, and "super-ego," meaning "above the ego" and referring to that aspect of our consciousness that is associated with ideals and visions.[19]

In its place we will use the term "personality." The word comes from the Greek word *persona*, meaning mask. It applies to

---

[19] Freud's student, Carl Jung, went off on his own and coined the terms "conscious," "subconscious" and "superconscious" mind to address the same distinctions. Modern psychologist Wayne Dyer, like Cady, ignores these forms. He uses the terms "small self" to refer to the sense-and-intellect-based mind and "Sacred Self" to refer to the Spirit-mind that is at the core of all.

the human part of you, the person, the external. Sometimes called the "carnal mind," it's governed by the intellect and senses.

When you say you don't like someone you mean you dislike their personality: the changeable exterior presentation of the person. *Personality is the outer, changeable person.*

Self, with a capital "S" is sometimes called the Christ Self, the Higher Self, the Inner Self, the true Self. It's the Spirit showing forth in us.

We shall use the term "individuality" in its place. Individuality comes from the Latin *individa*, meaning undividable. Our individuality is the undivided Self of God in us, and the more God comes into visibility through someone, the more individualized that person becomes.

DEVELOPING THE QUALITIES

Don't be confused: "coming through" does *not* mean "being religious." Instead, it refers to the visibility of the divine qualities of wisdom, love, power, etc. in their words and actions.

Ralph Waldo Emerson, whom we've quoted several times in this course, was a man of great individuality, but retiring personality. He was grandly simple in his daily life and modest in his public presentation. [20] But as much as his personality was willing to retire, the immortal God self of him, the individuality, shone even more brightly.

In the New Testament, John the Baptist and Judas Iscariot represent the illumined intellect. They represent personality, while Jesus typifies individuality. John recognized the superiority of Jesus and proclaimed Him; Judas felt betrayed by his Teacher's unwillingness to rely on personality and so betrayed Him.

While our personality tends to become like that of the people we associate with, our individuality never changes. It is the eternally unchanging Spirit-Self. It is that which ultimately distin-

---

[20] Emerson was a Unitarian minister who left the church and helped to found the Transcendentalist movement during the mid-1800s. He made his living writing provocative essays and delivering popular lectures.

guishes one person from another, no matter how similar they may appear.

A pronounced personality may be fearful or aggressive, fighting its way through obstacles and accomplishing much. But a pronounced individuality never battles; it's never puffed up with pride; it's never governed by likes and dislikes, and never causes them in others.[21] Personality bows before a pronounced individuality as the British Empire bowed before Gandhi, recognizing the impossibility of overcoming it.

We develop our individuality by listening to the "still, small voice" of loving acceptance deep within us, and boldly following it—even if it makes us different from others (which it definitely will, in the long run!). We develop personality by listening to voices outside ourselves and operating from fear—generating conceit, greed, fear of criticism, and neediness. They're mutually exclusive: as we cultivate individuality, personality decreases, along with all our fears.

One way to develop our own individuality, to identify with the Spirit Self within, is to focus on other peoples' Spirit, sometimes called the Christ, dwelling in every human being we meet. We can honor that Spirit, seeing through the mask of the personality to the love, wisdom, power, that resides in the heart of all beings. We can serve that Spirit by treating others with honor and respect, regardless of their position in the world. As we do so—as we love, honor, and serve Spirit manifest as individuality—we build our own individuality and less and less of our personality masks the Spirit dwelling in us.

RESPONDING TO STRONG PERSONALITIES

Whenever you avoid someone or feel afraid of them, it's because their personality is stronger than yours and overwhelms yours. Many timid people go through life believing that others are

---

[21] Gandhi's pronounced individuality led a nation to call him "Mahatma," which means "Great Soul." Mother Teresa's individuality led her to create a worldwide charitable order within the Roman Catholic Church when it was shutting down orders—and had her already being considered for sainthood, just weeks after her death.

better or wiser than they. They're afraid to meet a positive, self-possessed person, and when they do, they feel flattened, like grass after a storm; they wish they could get lost and stay lost, forever. All this happens, not because the other is wiser or better, but because their personality is stronger.

A timid person never feels this way in the presence of a strong individuality. Individuality in another not only generates our admiration, but also, when we're in their presence, gives us a new sense of our own possibilities, of exhilaration, comfort, and encouragement. This is because pronounced individuality has the power to call forth more of the same God-essence in others.

To avoid being overcome by someone's personality, *always remember that personality is only human, while individuality is divine.* Silently affirm your own individuality, your oneness with God—can God fear anyone?

BECOMING YOUR INDIVIDUAL SELF

If you're inclined to be timid or shrinking, practice the following. As you walk down the street and see anyone coming toward you, even a stranger, silently repeat "I am a part of God in visibility; I am one with the Father; this person has no power over me, for I am unaffected by personality." Make it a habit to repeat words like these whenever you approach someone, and you'll find that no personality, no matter how strong or aggressive, can throw you off balance. You will be Self-possessed; God-possessed.

If you find yourself bound to another personality, perhaps no longer even controlling your own thoughts, repeating the words above may make a difference but may not be sufficient. In our experience, declaring (silently), "There is no such personality in the universe as this one appears to be," and affirming it again and again over several days, leaves one feeling wondrously lifted, as if chains were dropping off.

In time, the voice within may urge us to go further, saying something like: "There is no personality in the universe; there is nothing but God!" After repeating these words a short time, every connection feels broken and one is free from that personality as if it never existed.

So, if at any time the lesser affirmations of Truth fail to free you from the influence of another personality, try the more sweeping one, "There is no personality, anywhere in the universe; there is nothing but God!" and you are bound to be free.

Always remember that God needs the individuality you are. You're part of the divine whole, with a unique role and place in the totality of All That Is. You're needed to manifest Spirit in your own special way. However humble your place in life, however unknown to the world you may be, however small your capacities may seem, you are just as necessary to the Wholeness of God as is the most brilliant intellect, the most beautiful, the most politically powerful person in the world.

Finally, act from the "still, small, voice"—the truest within you—to honor the highest, God's Spirit, within those around you. In time, you will realize that who you are is not a personality, but individuality, with all the wisdom, love, power, of Spirit manifesting through and as you.

SUMMARY

- Personality (usually called "ego" or "small self") is the outer, changeable person, a "mask" we put on to fit in with our environment.

- Our individuality (called the Higher Self, Christ Self, Buddha Nature, Spirit, and others) is the undivided Self of God in us: eternal, unchanging.

- A personality may be fearful or aggressive, fighting its way through obstacles and accomplishing much, but individuality never battles, is never puffed up with pride, never governed by likes and dislikes, and never causes those feelings in others.

- To avoid being overcome by someone's personality, always remember that personality is only human, while individuality is divine—can God fear anyone?

- We build our own individuality as we love, honor, and serve Spirit manifest as individuality in ourselves and others; then less and less of our personality masks the Spirit dwelling in us.

- We're each part of the divine whole, with a unique role and place in the totality of All That Is.

- In time, everyone will realize that who we are is not a personality, but individuality, with all the wisdom, love, power, of Spirit manifesting through and as each of us.

LESSON EIGHT: SPIRITUAL UNDERSTANDING

You can have an intellectual perception of Truth. You may easily grasp the statement that God is the giver of all good gifts—of life, health, love, power—just as people have for centuries. You may even go further, and intellectually see that God is not only the giver but the Gift—the life, health, love, power in us. But unless Truth is "revealed to you [by] my Father in Heaven," it's no use to you or to anyone else.

Jesus showed us this when his disciples answered a question confusedly, based on their perceptions, after which He asked them another, which Simon Peter answered clearly, based on intuition. In response, Jesus said: "Blessed are you, Simon bar Jonah, for flesh and blood did not reveal it to you; rather, it was my Father in Heaven" (Matthew 16:17).

Understanding is a spiritual transformation: a revelation of God's Wisdom within the human heart. Proverbs 3 and 4 speak eloquently to the point, comparing spiritual understanding to silver, gold, and rubies; calling the Wisdom of Spirit a tree of life and finally telling the reader, "With all thy getting, get understanding."

Only this revealed Truth brings about your desired healing. You may say to yourself, or someone else may say to you, over and over again, that you are wise and well and happy. On the mental level, a certain "cure" is achieved, and for a while you may feel well and wise and happy. But this is usually a form of hypnotism and is temporary.

Not until you feel your Oneness with the Father down in the depths of your being, not until you know within yourself that the fountain of all joy, wisdom and health is within your own being, ready to leap out the instant you call it forth, will you have spiritual understanding.

THE GOSPEL TEACHINGS

All the teachings of Jesus the Nazarene were designed to lead us into this awareness of oneness with the Father within. He had to begin with the external (people then, as now, being caught up with external things), and taught the people to love their enemies, do good to others, and so forth. These were external steps that led on to the state where desires are fulfilled. He told them they would find the kingdom of Heaven within themselves—the realm of all-love, all-power, all-beauty, all-joy. Finally Jesus said, "I have yet many things to say to you, but you cannot hear them now" (John 16:12).

At that point he told them of the Comforter he would leave them, which would teach them "all the deep things of God" (I Corinthians 2:10). Give them power over every form of sin, sickness, sorrow, and even death itself, and show them things to come.

The Comforter coming into the disciples' hearts and lives is what we mean by spiritual understanding.

The power that this consciousness of the indwelling Father gives is as much ours, today, as it was for the people Jesus was talking to. Perhaps more, for He said that those "who believe on me shall do the works that I do, and greater works also" (John 14:12).

REALIZATION

All the lessons in this course so far have also been stepping-stones, leading from doubt into faith, personality into individuality, up to the point where you may realize the ever-present inner-working Most High Creator. Paul, paraphrasing Jesus, understood: "Don't you know that your body is a temple of the Holy Spirit which is in you?" (I Corinthians 6:19).

No one can reveal the Creator to you. Nor can you reveal that Source to anyone else. If we've learned how, we may tell others how to seek and find Spirit working in themselves. But the actual realization, the new birth into the full awareness of our spiritual faculties and possibilities, takes place in the silence, the invisible—and in its own time. Jesus described it as like the wind that "blows where it will, and though you may hear its voice, you don't know where it came from or where it's going; so is everyone who is born of the Spirit" (John 3:8).

Spiritual understanding, our realization of the God-presence within, is, as Peter said, "the gift of God" (John 4:10). It's a gift that comes to any and all who seek it correctly. Hundreds of people have tried this method and have not received what they earnestly but ignorantly sought. They've not received because they don't know how to take what God freely offers.

In his essay explaining the divine experience, which he called "Over-Soul," Emerson said:

> This energy does not descend into individual life on any other condition than entire possession. It comes ... as insight; it comes as serenity and grandeur. When we see those whom it inhabits, we are apprised of new degrees of greatness. From that inspiration the man comes back with changed tone... does not want admiration; dwells in the hour that now is."

Others have not received this revelation because, as the apostle James wrote in one of his letters, "You ask and don't receive because you wish to spend it for selfish pleasure" (James 4:3).

Every human being wishes, whether they know it or not, for this new birth into a higher, spiritual consciousness. Everyone wants more good, more joy. And though unawakened minds may think they'll get those through more money or more things, what we all truly crave is more awareness of the presence of God, as all-good, always.

REVELATION: PARTIAL REALIZATION

It's possible for someone to want a partial revelation of God—say, as health—with all their heart. And, if they've learned how to take the desired gift (by uncompromising affirmation that it's theirs already), they *will* get realization of God as health. The same holds true with any of the "gifts of the Spirit:" healing, teaching the Good News, raising the dead, prophesying, casting out demons/passions, guiding on the path, providing for self and others, etc.

This is a step toward fulfillment. It's learning how to take God by faith for one's desires. But the time will come to every one of us when we'll hear the divine voice within say, "Come up higher!"

At that point, each of us will let go of any selfish desires that are just for our own comfort. *Each of us will desire more good just so we'll have more to give out,* knowing that as good flows through to others, it makes the person it's flowing through completely whole in the process. It fulfills them.

SEEK YE FIRST...

When David's son Solomon became king over Israel, the divine Presence appeared to him in a dream, saying "Ask what I shall give you." Solomon said, "Give your servant therefore an understanding heart that I might better guide your people" to this the Presence replied,

> Because you have asked this thing and not riches for yourself nor the life of your enemies, but have asked for understanding to discern justice, behold, I have done according to your word ... And have also given you what you haven't asked for, both riches and honor, so there shall be none among the kings like you, all your days (I Kings 3:5, 9-13).

By letting go of desire for all worldly goods, all merely selfish ends, and desiring only spiritual understanding, Solomon received all the other good things as well. Jesus taught the principle this way: "Seek ye first the kingdom ... and all these things shall be added" (Matthew 6:33).

On that day when, more than riches and honor and power and selfish glory, you desire spiritual understanding for its own sake; on that day will come to you the revelation of God within you, and you shall become aware of and identify with the indwelling Father, who is life and strength and power and peace. As the prophets of old were told, "If with all your hearts you truly seek me, you shall ever surely find me" (Jer. 29:13).

STAGES IN THE PROCESS

When you first consciously desire spiritual understanding, you'll probably not immediately attain it. After all, you've been living in the external world of your being—our culture—and have, at some level at least, thought yourself cut off from God.

The first step is to say, like the Prodigal Son, "I will arise and go to my Father's house" (Luke 15:18). At that point you can turn your thoughts away from the external appearance and toward the center, the Reality. You can begin to know, intellectually, that you are not separate from God and that the Divine always desires to manifest Its Self within you and through you as your freedom from all suffering.

Then, as Jesus taught his disciples, we begin to lop off any branches of selfishness. We try to love instead of hate; to forgive instead of avenging ourselves; to deny the emotions of envy, jealousy, greed, anger, and the beliefs in sickness, evil, and pain that no longer serve us. We affirm love, peace, health, supply, and support in a universe that is free from fear.

As we move along the path, we begin to speak the words of Truth that are presented in this course and related materials, even though we may only grasp them intellectually. This is the light in the darkness that will help us and others in a world of dark ignorance.

As with all journeys, there will be times when you will feel almost overcome with doubts and questions—especially when you look for results that aren't there. But you must continue through this "valley of the shadow," this "long dark night." It's part of the process and, like the Israelites wandering in the wilderness, we all go through it.

Along the way, we discover that faithful service for others speeds up the process. Many who've been earnestly seeking spiritual understanding have felt an unselfish desire to help others once they've found the power of God within. But this "gift of God" comes to us more or less quickly as we use the light we already have. The gifts of God are not rewards for faithful service, but service is one of the steps that lead to the place where our fulfillment awaits us. We grow by sharing with others the light and knowledge we have.

Is not this the fast that I have chosen: to loose the bonds of wickedness, to undo the bands of the yoke and to let the oppressed go free? Is it not to deal thy bread to the hungry, and bring the poor that are cast out to thy house? When you see the naked, that you cover him? ... then your light shall break forth as the morning, and your healing shall spring forth ...Then you shall call and the Creator will answer ... "Here I am" (Isaiah 58:6-11)

We do this knowing, and feeling, the full support, love, and power of God is working through us, keeping the fountain flowing from that deep reservoir within.

So, as was discussed in the first lesson, we don't abstain from pleasure, or even deny ourselves in service. Too much fasting becomes starvation, damaging the body and mind for lack of nutrients. Too much study or meditation overwhelms the soul. We are fountains that must have an inlet and outlet if we are to remain clear.

Then, some day, in the fullness of God's time, while you are using these words of Truth, they'll suddenly become the living Word "made flesh" in you—the power will come through the words. Then you'll no longer dwell in darkness, for the light within your own heart, your own enlightenment, will invest your world with a new life and understanding. You'll become aware of a new, more divine life in your body, more love in your heart, and more power in your soul to accomplish your good.

You'll no longer run around looking to teachers or healers for their guidance. The Scriptures have new meaning as the Spirit of Truth reveals to you "the deep things of God."

This is Spiritual Understanding. This is when you will no longer care about others' opinion nor seek their admiration, but speak plain and true, simply sharing the eternal Wisdom flowing through you—and delighting in the gifts thereof.

SUMMARY

- Understanding is a spiritual transformation: a revelation of God's Wisdom within the human heart.

- When you feel your Oneness with the Father down in the depths of your being, when you know within yourself that the fountain of all joy, wisdom and health is within your own being, ready to leap out the instant you call it forth, you will have spiritual understanding.

- All the teachings of Jesus the Nazarene were designed to lead us into this awareness of oneness with the Father within.

- No one can reveal the Creator to another. If we've learned how, we may tell others how to seek and find Spirit working in themselves.

- People have tried this method and have not received what they earnestly but ignorantly sought because they don't know how to take what God freely offers or because they're asking for selfish reasons.

- The first step is to turn our thoughts away from the external appearance toward the Reality at our core.

- There are times when you feel almost overcome with doubts and questions, but you must continue through this "valley of the shadow;" it's part of the process.

- We grow by sharing with others the light and knowledge we have, knowing and feeling the full support, love, and power of God working through us.

- One day, in the fullness of God's time, while you are using these words of Truth, they'll suddenly become the living Word "made flesh" in you—the power will come through the words; this is Spiritual Understanding.

LESSON NINE: THE SECRET PLACE OF THE MOST HIGH

There is nothing the human heart longs for as much as to know God.

People shift from one thing to another, always hoping to find rest and satisfaction in some anticipated accomplishment or possession. They think they want houses and lands, knowledge and power. They pursue these things and gain them, only to find themselves restless again, still unsatisfied.

Deep in our hearts is a great and awful homesickness that has never been and can never be satisfied with anything less than a clear, vivid experience of the indwelling Presence, our Father-Mother God.

In all ages, earnest men and women who have recognized this hunger as the heart's calling for God have left striving for things. They've done all they can to bring about this experience through devoted worship and service to others. Few, however, have succeeded in reaching the place where their joy is full. Still others have gone back and forth, trying to "work out" their "own salvation" without realizing that there must be an inworking as well as an outworking: "it is the gift of God, not of works" (Eph 2: 9).

You may study with human teachers and from man-made books until doomsday; you may get all the theology of the ages; you may understand intellectually all the statements of Truth and be able to quote healing formulas as smoothly as oil flows. Still, until there is a definite inner revealing of the indwelling Spirit through whom and by whom comes all life, health, peace, and power—in truth, is all these and more—you have not yet found "the secret place of the Most High" (Psalm 91).

In that place, the psalm tells us, we have immunity from all "deadly pestilence" and the "snare of the fowler," from "the terror by night" and the "arrow that flies by day" (Psalm 91). We've even been promised freedom from the fear of those things!

SEEKING THE PLACE

Where is this place? Where can we find it?

"The Secret place of the Most High," where we are free from all fear or trouble, is the point of mystical union between human and Spirit—called the Christ among Christians and the Buddha-nature, the Tao, or *Samadhi* in the Eastern traditions.

There we no longer believe, but know that God abides always at the center of our being as our perfect well-being, ready to come into manifestation the moment we claim it. We *feel* it. We feel our oneness with the Father and we manifest that oneness.

In order to find this place, this understanding, this awareness of God within themselves, many have been willing to spend all they possess. It's the "pearl of great price" in the ancient story. Paul, after twenty-five years of powerful preaching and teaching across the Roman Empire, said, "I count all things as nothing compared to the excellence of knowing Christ" (Philippians 3:8).

Yet this understanding can't be found through the intellect. It's not perceivable through the senses, thoughts, or emotions.

What we seek is a direct revelation of the living Presence within us, of divine Power moving through us, creating Good in our world—for who can give us the secret that is the key to all power, except the "Spirit of Truth, which proceeds from the Father?" (John 15:26). The Creator-Sustainer of our being, which is the power of our universe, must whisper the secret to each one of us. And that which God would say to you is a secret that no other can know—it can't even be put into human language! So each human being, must, when all's said and done, experience the Christ center, or Buddha-nature, to come into the knowledge that we all seek.

The gospel stories following the resurrection illustrate this process. Mary, called the Magdalene, had assisted the Master for years. Still, when she spoke with the man outside the tomb, she assumed he was the gardener—until he "spoke her name" and she, in a flash of intuition, recognized her Teacher. Similarly, Thomas Didymus had walked daily with Jesus for three years, eaten with Him, listened to Him and spoken with Him. He had all the metaphysical training you and I have had, and more. But his intellect wasn't enough. Nor were his senses. It was an inner re-vealing that made him cry out, "My Lord and my God!" (John 20:28).

The revelation never comes through the intellect, but through the intuition *to* the intellect. "The natural man receives not the things of the Spirit of God, for they are foolishness to him and he cannot know them..." Paul tells us in his letter to the Corinthians (I Corinthians 2:14).

NEITHER BOOKS NOR TEACHERS

In our eagerness to experience our hearts' desire, we've reached for every source we could find for the light we seek. Not knowing how to wait in the silence, we've run around trying to find it in others' teachings.

But you must forget the notion that you can come to this place through any other human being. No outside person can ei-ther induct you or enter into it for you. No one can come into it from the outside. No teacher can find it for you.[22]

Now, books and teachers are useful, up to a point. "How shall they hear without a preacher?" (Romans 10:14). Paul devoted his life to waking people up to the possibility, but even he knew he couldn't go there for them. And Jesus, himself, said "I will ask the Father and He will give you another Comforter [the Holy Spirit], and He will never leave you." (John 14:16). He knew He had to leave his disciples if they were ever to come to their own realization. Had the Master remained with the disciples, it's doubt-ful whether they'd ever have gone beyond hanging onto his words, trying to figure them out. He knew that each of us must, on our own, wait upon God for the inner illumination, the enlightenment, that is lasting and real.

There comes a time for each of us when we must learn for ourselves that the Spirit lives in us; that God within us is our life and light and all good. When your intellect has grasped that, you cease looking to teachers outside of you to bring you spiritual in-

---

[22] The Hindu tradition of *guru* is a process of first placing all one's desire on an outside person, who then shows one how to go inside and find it; the Buddhists say the *guru* is within.

sight. Teachers may talk about the light, but the light itself must flash in the darkness for you to see it.

This is a gift our Father-Mother, Creator-Sustainer God longs with an infinite longing to reveal to each of us. God's desire to show us the secret is the seed of our desire for the revelation.

THE EXPERIENCE

When we say we receive these gifts from God "on high," we're saying they come from a higher region of consciousness, a higher vibration of being, than our normal waking minds. They come through our individuality, not our personality. The Holy (which means whole, entire, complete) Spirit must descend into our soul, our mind. It must lower its vibration from pure light to visible light. And we must raise our vibration to meet it. This is the only way we can experience the enlightenment (meaning light-filled mind) that we seek.

When you have learned how to raise your own awareness to that level and abandon yourself to infinite spirit, and do so daily, you'll be amazed at the change in you. You'll become aware of light, life, love, and all good, perfectly filling any sense of lack while you simply wait quietly and receive.

Paul, who learned this way of faith, of being still and letting the I Am work into his conscious mind as the fulfillment of his desires, spoke of it often in his letters. He received daily and served willingly, often praying that others would receive as well:

> I bow my knees unto the Father ... that He would grant unto you the riches of His glory, that you may be strengthened with power ... that you, being rooted and grounded in love, may ... know the love of Christ that is beyond knowledge, that you may be filled with all the fullness of God, by the power that works in us (Ephesians 3:14-20).

And to this we say, *Amen.*[23]

---

23 "Amen" is an ancient word with rich meaning: "so be it; it is so; on this ground I stand and have my being;" "on this I stand and from henceforth move forward."

SUMMARY

- Deep in our hearts is a great and awful homesickness that has never been and can never be satisfied with anything less than a clear, vivid experience of the indwelling Presence, our Father-Mother God.

- "The Secret place of the Most High," where we are free from all fear or trouble, is the point of mystical union between human and Spirit.

- There comes a time for each of us when we must learn for ourselves that the Spirit lives in us; that God within us is our life and light and all good.

- Revelation never comes through the intellect, but through the intuition *to* the intellect.

- When you've learned how to raise your own awareness and abandon yourself to infinite spirit, and do so daily, you'll become aware of light, life, love, and all good, perfectly filling any sense of lack while you simply wait quietly and receive.

LESSON TEN: FINDING THE SECRET PLACE

How to seek the Secret Place—where to find it—how to abide in it—these are the questions that today, more than any time in history,[24] are in our hearts. More than anything else, this knowledge, this *experience* is what we seek. And in this experience all other desires are fulfilled.

OUR DESIRE IS IN GOD

If you wanted my love or anything that I am (rather than I *have*), you wouldn't go ask Tom, Dick, or Mary to get it. They might tell you that I could or would give of myself, but ultimately you would have to come to me.

So it is with Spirit. We must go to God, as Spirit within us, for the light and love we seek, because God doesn't *have* these things; God *is* these things, and dwells within each of us waiting to manifest more of them as us and through us.

We don't need to be anxious or concerned, though. Let's not lose sight of the fact that our desire, great as it is, truly is God's desire for us. "No one can come to me unless the Father that sent me draws him" (John 6:44). The Father-Mother Spirit in us must desire to reveal the secret, or we wouldn't feel the hunger for it, the drive to discover the Truth.

Whoever and wherever you are in life, remember that the Christ Spirit, speaking through Jesus, said "You did not choose me, but I chose you, and appointed you to go forth and bear fruit" (John 6:44). Whether you are preparing to preach the Gospel, to heal the sick, or simply to live a more fulfilling life, *know that your seeking is Spirit reaching out to you.* Your longing is the same eternal energy that causes the planets to orbit always seeking to manifest itself more fully.

You need not worry nor strive. You need only to let it work.

---

[24] And she wrote this over 100 years ago!

GOING TO THE SOURCE

In these lessons so far, we've been learning how to do the outworking that makes us ready, but now we must learn how to set our inner awareness so we can experience the divine inner working.

So, if you've been working with the intellect and sensory perceptions, it's now time to shift your approach to the one Jesus taught and "become as little children" (Matthew 18:3). It's time to allow the Father-Mother Presence to speak to you through your intuition. It's time to "be still and know." The light that you crave will come out of the deep, inner silence and become manifest to you from within yourself—if you will but sit silently, "waiting on the Lord."

Most of us have no idea how to "wait ... in silence for God only" (Psalm 62:5). "Sitting in the silence" doesn't mean very much to people who only know how to listen to external voices. But sound and noise are reflections in the environment; Spirit is the Truth within. God works in stillness and we can learn to be aware of that silent working.

A story by Edward Everett Hale tells of a little girl playing among the birds and butterflies in a country village. Frequently, she would stop and run into the chapel to pray. Then she'd sit quietly for a few minutes "waiting," she said, "to see if God wanted to say anything." We can do the same.

GUIDELINES FOR WAITING

"Sitting in the silence" is not some sort of lazy drifting. It's a passive, but definite waiting upon God. It's not begging or pleading or supplicating God for some favor or gift. It's knowing that the gift is on its way and expecting to receive it momentarily. And it's best begun alone, in an undisturbed time and place.

Take a time when you won't be disturbed. Close the door, turn off the phone and other devices that might interrupt, and, if necessary close the blinds or curtains.

Practice alone, undisturbed, until you can enter the Silence easily and feel the Presence without being affected by what's going on around you.

Begin by lifting your heart in praise and thanksgiving to the all-loving, all-giving Father-Mother Creator-Sustainer of all being. This helps center our awareness in the higher Presence and counteracts the tendency of the human mind to run around in trivial thoughts and concerns.

Many people, wanting to experience the silence have found their minds taking off in all directions at once—the natural result of trying to "stop thinking." Nature abhors a vacuum, and if you try to make your mind a vacuum natural processes will fill it back up again.

You can prevent this disturbance by filling your mind with higher thoughts—of the glories and wonders of God.

Some people use prayer to elevate their awareness. Of course prayer doesn't change God's attitude toward us, but it's easier for us to take a few steps toward a higher elevation than a great leap. So we can say favorite lines from psalms or hymns, like *"Oh God, our help in ages past, our hope for years to come..."* Or from Isaiah, made familiar in Handel's *Messiah: "For He shall reign for ever and ever; King of kings, Lord of lords, forever!"* Prayerful words that work for some include, *"God's will is my greatest desire working in me now."* Or if that's too much for you to accept, step back a bit and say something like, *"Let your Life flow through me now,"* or *"Let the divine will, which is all good, be done in me."*

No set words are needed, but whatever words you use, repeat them many times, relaxing, not straining—and definitely not reaching out and away to an outside God.

Some people work so hard to reach out and upward for God that you can see it in their faces. They haven't learned yet that they simply need to go into their own hearts to find what they seek. You don't want to reach out like that; it doesn't work. If a seed were planted in the earth and reached only for the sun above, there would be no root system to support it and give it nourishment.

Some people, working to reach up to God, make the mistake of climbing right out of their bodies. This abnormal stretching is wearing on the body, leaving it weak and cold. We know better than to seek outside for the Spirit; instead, we go within and let the Son-light draw us upward as fast as we can be strong in the light.

While waiting upon Spirit, relax as much as possible—mentally and physically. Let yourself be like a gull, drying on the sand, consciously absorbing all the light and warmth that is there.

Let your words become a quiet, caring, lifting up of the heart to a higher something within yourself, to what Jesus called "the Father in me" (John 14:11). Let them be said with the quiet assurance of a child speaking to a loving parent or grandparent. You can say something like:

> I know that You live within me; that You are alive here, now. You have all power; you're the answer to all I desire. I know that You radiate from the center of my being to fill my body, and beyond, throughout the world as the fulfillment of my desire.

While you're focusing this way on God, in conversation with the Spirit within, no other kinds of thoughts can possibly rush in; your mind is open only to God.

THE FULFILLMENT OF DESIRES

Now, in that restful, relaxed place, believe that what you have called forth is being done. Know that divine Substance is flowing in at the center and out into the manifest world every minute. Know that Substance *does* come forth in the form of your desire as you expect it to.

If you find your mind wandering, bring it right back in focus by saying something like, "*It is being done; Beloved Spirit, You work in me now; I am receiving all that my heart desires.* Don't look for signs and wonders; just be still and know that the very thing you seek is flowing in and will come forth into manifestation. It may be immediately, or, if you have conflicting feelings or thoughts, it may take a while, but it is done.

So, knowing it is as you have wished, go beyond. Give thanks to the indwelling Presence for hearing and responding, for coming forth into visibility as your desire. There's something about the act of thanksgiving that moves the mind beyond all doubt and into the clarity of faith and trust where "all things are possible."

Even if you aren't yet aware of receiving anything, give thanks. Don't worry. Don't think of going back and asking again, but continue to give thanks that while you waited you received, and that what you received in Spirit is now manifest in Substance. You'll soon be rejoicing in gratitude for the fulfillment of your desire!

When you feel un-well, "wait thou in silence for God only" (Psalm 62:5), rather than waiting upon healers.

When you seek wisdom in large or small matters "wait thou in silence for God only," just as you would for any teacher or counselor, and see what wonderful wisdom for action is yours.

When you desire to speak the word that will deliver someone from the bondage of sickness, sin, pain, or sorrow, "wait thou in silence for God only," and exactly the right word will be given to you—and power with it, for it will be alive with the power of Spirit.

A caveat: *Don't let waiting in the silence be a burden!* If you find yourself straining, get up and do something else for a while. Or, if your mind insists on wandering, don't insist on concentrating; a rigid mindset shuts off the flow. There must be a sort of relaxed expectancy, a comfortable readiness to "take by faith."

MORE THAN WAITING

There are those who, in their desire to find that secret place and experience enlightenment, are always seeking the light for themselves, neglecting to use what they already have in service to others. They will not succeed.

There must be an equal, conscious receiving from Spirit and giving out to the world—a perfect equilibrium between inflowing and outflowing—to keep balance and harmony. We must each learn how to wait upon God for the inflowing and then give out to every creature that which we've received—as Spirit leads us to give: in preaching, teaching, healing, nurturing, or silently living the Truth.

Jesus didn't spend all his time in receiving. When He spent many hours alone in communion with the Father his greatest works were done after these long sessions. He poured forth into the everyday lives of all around him all that He received. And we must do likewise, for our new life and revelation flows in as fast as we give it out in service to others.

Fortunately, the light that fills us radiates from us without effort, right where we are. Spirit will root out abilities that you're barely aware of, simply because they've been waiting there, silently, for the opportunity to be expressed. Serving becomes as easy as breathing; love becomes your Way.

EXPERIENCING THE TOTALITY

In time, as we grow in spiritual understanding, we begin to want, more than anything else, to experience infinite love and wisdom fulfilled in us. Yet, we discover, as Isaiah did,

> My thoughts are not your thoughts; neither are your ways my ways, says Yahweh. For as the heavens are higher than (encompassing) the earth, so are my ways higher (more inclusive) than your ways and my thoughts higher than your thoughts (Isaiah 55:8).

Our desires are always God's desires, but until now, in a limited way. As we see that more of God means more good and joy and happiness, we soon throw aside those self-imposed limitations.

Then we find ourselves crying out in the silence, "Fulfill Your highest thought in me, now!" At that moment we make ourselves clay in the potter's hands, willing to be re-shaped, re-molded, "transformed into the same image" (II Corinthians 3:18) as Christ, one with the indwelling Spirit.

As we enter into this deeper process, we find ourselves saying something like

> Holy Spirit, You are renewing me according to Your highest thought for me; You are radiating your very Self through my entire being, making me one with You, manifesting as You, in Your image—for there is none else but You, dearest Father-Mother Spirit. Thank You! Thanks be always and everywhere!

Then be still while Spirit works.

While you're waiting, letting the Spirit work, marvelous changes will be made in you. You'll have a wonderful new consciousness of peace: serenity. You'll feel something has been done, that some new power to overcome has come to you.

One touch of the Oversoul makes all life seem different! All the hard things become easy; the troublesome things are no longer worth worrying over; the annoying people and events of the world no longer matter. We no longer have to deny evil; we know in that moment that evil is nothing at all. We no longer discipline ourselves to affirm the good—we can't help it! Faith has become a reality. We consciously receive from the Source the power and understanding that lets us "speak the word" and make perfection immediately visible.

At that moment, you'll be comfortable saying the powerful words, "I and the Father are one" with a new meaning, a new sense of reality, and a new awe that will make you feel very still—as did Jesus when he experienced the same divine union. For the time, you'll comprehend and appreciate what the Spirit experiences; "seeing" as God "sees."

You may not get all these results immediately. Don't be discouraged. Every moment that you wait, Spirit is working to make you a new being—one who consciously has divine qualities and powers. There may be several days on inner working before you see the change (the gospels tell us Jesus spent 40 days in the wilderness before he felt ready), but it will surely come.

And, as with anything else, with practice you'll get to the point where you can go into the silence—into conscious communion with God—at a moment's notice. Any time. Any place.

ABIDING IN THE PRESENCE

This clear revelation, God's word made alive as Truth in our awareness, *must* come to every one who continues to wait upon God—as long as the seeker meets two conditions.

First, we are to abide, which means to *dwell* "in the secret place of the Most High" (Psalm 91:1), not merely run in and out. Of course this doesn't mean you're to spend all your time in meditation and silence but that your mind is continually in an attitude of waiting upon God. That is, continually listening for the still, small voice of Spirit, wherever you are—not clamoring for attention but being ready to receive.

The second essential condition is expectation—expecting to feel the Presence, to see the works. Is your expectation from the Creator-Sustainer of the Universe, or from books, teachers, friends, classes, meetings, or loved ones? "Truly in vain is the help that is looked for from the hills...truly in Yahweh our God is the salvation..." (Jeremiah 3:23); "Yahweh your God is in your midst" (Zephaniah 3:15). In *your* midst—at the center of your being at this very moment, while you read these words!

> Yahweh thy God is in your midst, a mighty one who will save;
> He will rejoice over you; He will be quiet in His love; He will ex-
> ult over you with singing" (Zephaniah 3:15-17).

You are God's love! You are rejoiced over! As you turn away from other resources and toward the Spirit within you, God's singing and joy will fill you so that your life will be a great thanksgiving!

Your Own Father-Mother, Creator-Sustainer Lord

"Thy God" is yours alone. Your Lord is not my Lord. Your Lord is the Christ Spirit within your being; my Lord is the Spirit in my being—unique to me.

There is one Spirit, one Father-Mother, one Oversoul expressing itself in and through all creation. But there are different manifestations, or aspects of that One: different individualities.

Your Lord is the Spirit that delivers you out of all your troubles. Your own Mother-Father God has no other business but to manifest in and through you, and so make you whole with divine health; mighty with divine power; perfectly manifesting the perfection of the Christ. As Jesus experienced God as His own dear "Daddy" (*Abba*), you will experience your own loving Presence, yours alone.

So let all your communion be with your own loving Presence. Let all your expectation be for your own God of might. Wait upon Spirit dwelling within you, expecting great things, now.

SUMMARY

- We must go to Spirit within us for the light and love we seek, because Spirit *is* these things, and dwells within each of us waiting to manifest more of them as us and through us.

- God, as Spirit, works in stillness and we can learn to be aware of that silent working.

- When you enter into conversation with the Spirit within, no other kinds of thoughts can possibly rush in; your mind is open only to God.

- In that restful, relaxed place, believe that what you have claimed is being done; know that divine Substance comes forth in the form of your desire as you expect it to.

- The act of thanksgiving moves the mind beyond all doubt and into the clarity of faith and trust.

- We must each wait upon God for the inflowing and then give out to every creature that which we've received—as Spirit leads us to serve.

- As we see that more of God means more good and joy and happiness, we become willing to be "transformed into the same image" (II Corinthians. 3:18) as Christ, one with the indwelling Spirit.

- There is one Spirit expressing itself in and through all creation, but there are different manifestations, or aspects of that One; That aspect dwelling within you is your own.

Lesson Eleven: Gifts of the Spirit

It's natural for people to set out in search of Truth because of the material rewards (healings, "loaves and fishes," etc.). In fact, it may be that *most* people first turn to God because of some weakness, some failure, or some unbearable need in their lives. After trying everything else in vain, they turn in desperation to God.

Everyone wants to be free of their ills, free of all suffering. Some realize they want to be free from all forms of distress, free as the birds of the air. And we have a right to be; it's a God-given desire—and a God-given right.

Even the most depraved human being (though he wouldn't admit it for the world!) instinctively feels that there's a power somewhere that can give him just what he wants, and if only he could reach that power, he could prevail upon it to grant the things he desired. This feeling is itself God-given. It's the divine spark at the center of his being suggesting a remedy for all his ills.

Many Gifts

In the early days of the practice of Truth, all teaching was limited to the manifestation of infinite Love as healing.[25]

For centuries, sickness, seemingly incurable disease, and suffering were everywhere and every sufferer wanted to be free. We didn't know that there was willingness and power—even intense desire—on the part of the indwelling Spirit to give us something more than sweet, patient submission to suffering.

When at first the truth was taught that the divine Presence lives in all beings as perfect Life and can be drawn upon by our recognition and faith into the experience of perfect well-being, the

---

[25] The earliest teachings of this science were offered by a healer, Phineas P. Quimby of Belfast, Maine, who believed he had found the means by which Jesus had accomplished his healings. A patient and student of his, Dr. Mary Baker Patterson, went on to become the Rev. Mrs. Eddy, the founder of the Church of Christ, Scientist, known today as "Christian Science."

teaching attracted widespread attention, as it should. Both teachers and students focused on this one outcome, and lost sight of the larger, fuller, deeper, more complete manifestation of the indwelling Father-Mother that is possible.

Time has shown us, though, that there are many more gifts, and a much greater Truth to be experienced.

Why should we limit the limitless one to a single gift? Only if we're so consumed with desire for that one that we're sure it's God's desire for us—in which case it flows forth effortlessly through our faith. Even in a crowd of people, without any effort on our part, the one who needs healing will "touch" us, as the woman in the multitude is said to have touched Jesus' cloak (Matthew 9:21).

Healing is truly a "branch" of the "vine" (John 15:4), but it's not the only branch. There are many, all of which are essential for the perfect vine—which is seeking through each of us to bear fruit.

Paul told the Christians at Corinth about these gifts:

...there are diversities of gifts but the same Spirit ... For to one is given through the Spirit the word of wisdom, and to another the word of knowledge, according to the same Spirit to another faith ... to another gifts of healings ... to another workings of miracles, and to another prophecy, and to another discerning of spirits; to another diverse tongues, and to another the interpretation of tongues (I Corinthians 12: 4, 8-10).

The same Spirit, always one and forever the same—one Spirit, one God—but in different forms of manifestation. All equally important to the whole.

What God wants is for all of us to grow into such a conscious union with Spirit, such realization of the Source of all-good dwelling within us, that we can be sure that "Ask what you will and it shall be done for you" (John 15:7).

To Each Our Own

Let's all focus on our own work, our own God, our own gifts. And if you're faithfully and sincerely living what Truth you know and still lack the healing power (or abundant supply, or clarity of vision), call it good. Rest assured; no matter what anyone else says or thinks, this apparent lack simply means that you need to let go of that single gift and go for the whole set.

Don't for a moment be afraid to let go of the one little branch! Choose instead to have the highest thoughts of Infinite Mind, whatever they may be, fulfilled through you. We need to take our hands off the single branches and focus on the whole vine.

You are here for some particular purpose. If, when the time comes, you let loose, cheerfully, of the grasp you've kept on one particular form of manifesting, and "desire earnestly the greater gifts" (I Corinthians. 12:31), whatever Spirit may bring forth through you, you'll do marvelous works through them. More, these works will happen without any effort on your part, because they'll be Spirit, the omnipotent omnipresence within you, manifesting through you.

It's all the same Spirit. To be the greatest success, you don't want my gifts, nor do I want yours. We each want our own, to fit our capacity and desires, as the Spirit in us chooses.

Seek fulfillment in the Spirit if you want to experience the greater gifts. Spirit will reveal to you the specific set of gifts that is God's perfect manifestation through your perfect being.

FEAR NOT

Why should we fear to wait with perfect willingness for the Spirit to manifest itself through us as it will? Why are so many afraid to let go? Have we not seen God's works and called them good? Then why are so many afraid to abandon themselves to the workings of infinite love and wisdom?

We know that whatever the manifestation, it will be good—all good—to ourselves and to those around us!

The courage to let go of our opinion and accept God's is rare, indeed. And for some, acting on such courage might mean an apparent downward turning of whatever success they may have achieved in the past. But such a turning could only lead to a wonderful soaring upward, a resurrection of the Christ Spirit into visibility through you!

So don't fear failure, but call apparent failure good, for it really is. Didn't Jesus, to all appearances, stand as an utter failure when He stood before Pilate? But if He hadn't seemed to fail right at that point, there couldn't have been in infinitely grander demonstration of His resurrection later on.

The apparent failure of the moment can only mean a grand success, later on.[26]

BEYOND LIMITS

Your greatest work will be done through your own God-appointed channel. If you will let Spirit possess your will completely, if you will to have the highest will done in you and through you continually, you will be quickly moved out of your present limitations.

These limitations, indicated by your current partial successes, will fall away as a fuller and more perfect manifestation comes forth—as much fuller and more perfect as new grain is, compared to the old seed that had to fall to the ground and die.

Old ways must die. Failure is only the death of the old so there may be a hundredfold increase. If, at any time, a gift you've been using no longer "works" for you, allow someone else to work it for you and know that, right here, there is something even better, waiting for you to call it forth.

The Holy Spirit, which is God in motion, wants to open a bigger, brighter way for you. Any apparent failure is God's call to you to stop what you've been doing and turn your attention inward. "Acquaint yourself now with Him and be at peace, so good shall come to you" (Job 22:21). Turn to the divine Presence within you. Seek the Spirit. Be still before your God. Wait upon your Lord quietly, sincerely, expectantly and continually—for days and weeks if necessary!

If, when these transition periods come (in which, through "failure," God would lead us higher), we become frightened or

---

[26] How many people have looked back at an apparent failure and declared it "the best thing that ever happened to me?" How many businesses have failed only to be replaced with one infinitely better? Failure in the world of Spirit's Creation is not an option.

discouraged, we miss the opportunity Spirit is offering us—and postpone the day of receiving our own fullest, highest gift. In our ignorance and fear we would be hanging onto the old grain of wheat, not daring to let it fall into the ground, so there would be no resurrection, no fullness of life, no limitless increase in our capacity.

Let Spirit work in you and, sooner or later, you will spring up into a resurrected life of newness and power beyond anything you've dreamed of before.

THE WAY AND THE LIFE

Clearly, we must learn to no longer fear God.[27] We must come to know the loving Presence within ourselves. We must stop focusing on the information of our senses and seek to live a life in partnership with Spirit.[28] We must begin, truly, to embody the Christ, to be in union with the Spirit that dwells within our being, and to teach others to do the same.

"I am the way, the Truth and the Life" (John 14:6), said the Christ embodied as Jesus. So says the Spirit in you, as well. Do you see that your first—your continual—thought is really only to seek life in the Spirit, to seek knowing the Presence as a living reality? After that, ask what you will, be it power to heal, to cast out demons, or even the "greater works" that Jesus promised we should do (John 14:2), and "it shall be done unto you" (John 15:7).

---

[27] One of Dr. Cady's teachers. Emma Curtis Hopkins, said that the word that has been translated as "fear" regarding God, really means to "have a single eye" to "remain focused on" as one would with anything that inspired awe and fascination.

[28] When Dr. Cady was writing, the owner of a dress shop was having a difficult time and "went into his closet" to find the solution. The result was a new kind of partnership and decades of success for his business, now named "Lord and Taylor."

SUMMARY

- Many people are afraid to abandon themselves to the workings of infinite love and wisdom, but we know that whatever the manifestation, it will be good—all good—to ourselves and to those around us!

- Any apparent failure is God's call to you to stop what you've been doing and turn your attention inward.

- Your greatest work will be done through your own God-appointed channel.

- Spirit will reveal to you the specific set of gifts that is God's perfect manifestation through your perfect being.

- Let Spirit work in you and, sooner or later, you will spring up into a resurrected life of newness and power beyond anything you've dreamed of before!

LESSON TWELVE: UNITY OF THE SPIRIT

It would be easy to get discouraged in this world if we didn't know as a living reality that, behind all the variety of human understandings, is one Mind. Behind all, the master Artist is, through human hands, putting a touch of color here, another there, seeing the end from the beginning.

From time immemorial there have been schisms and divisions among religious sects and denominations. And still today, with all the knowledge we have of one God abiding in all humanity, too many still cling to cultural differences.

It's as if people were living inside a wall, a wall with a few small openings, and each of them, looking through their narrow slit were saying, "I see the whole world!" Of course, each would see only some of what was beyond the wall and all would be convinced the others were wrong—and all would be correct, at least partially.

BREAK DOWN THE WALLS

It's time to break down the seeming "middle wall of partition" as Paul called it (Ephesians 2:14), as the living Christ breaks down all misunderstanding. It's time to see that *there is no real wall of difference between the various sects of theology*, only those that appear because of a limited viewpoint. It's time to understand that every attempt to limit God's manifestation of Spiritual Substance in anyone or through anyone in order to make that manifestation conform to your idea of truth, you're simply demonstrating your ignorance.

It's time to lose sight of all differences, all side-issues, and seek for one thing only: the awareness of the Presence of the indwelling Spirit. And, just as there is less separation between the spokes of a wheel as you approach the center, you'll find that the nearer you come to the Perfection at your core, the less difference you'll see between you and others.

The happy person who exclaims "Praise the Lord!" from his heart, no matter what occurs to him, finds with Paul that "to them

83

that love God all things work in good" (Romans 8::28). Such a one is actually saying the metaphysician's "all is good." The metaphysician, therefore, whether from Unity, Religious Science, Divine Science, or any other metaphysical school, need not look down on the Pentecostal, charismatic, or orthodox Christian.

A woman spoke in an orthodox Christian prayer meeting, knowing no more of metaphysical science than a baby knows of Greek. Her face, however, was radiant with the light of the Christ manifest through her. She told how, five or six years before, she had been asking to know more of God through prayer, and one day, in all earnestness, had asked that some special word of His be given her as a sort of private message. The words flashed on her mind: "If therefore thine eye be single, thy whole body shall be full of light ... no man can serve two masters" (Matthew 6:24). The woman had read these words many times before but that day they were illumined by Spirit, and she knew that to have a "single" eye meant seeing only one power in her life. As long as she saw two powers (God and devil, good and evil) she was serving two masters. From that day forward, though she had passed through all sorts of difficulties, she always found the most marvelous whole and complete deliverance out of them. As she put it, "Lookin' at God with one eye and this evil with the other is bein' double-eyed, and God told me to keep my eye single."

This woman, who had never heard of any science or metaphysical teachings or laws of Mind was overcoming the tribulations of this world by positively refuting to have any but a single eye. She'd been taught in a single flash of insight by infinite Spirit the whole secret of how to banish every distress and have only good and joy. Isn't it wonderfully simple?

The teachings of Spirit are intrinsically the same, because Spirit is one. At the center, all is one and the same God, forevermore.

Even someone who worships the golden calf as his highest conception of the divine worships God. His mind has not yet been expanded to a state where he can grasp any idea of God beyond the physical form: something he can see with human eyes and touch with human hands. But at heart he seeks something greater than his present conscious self to be his deliverance out of distress.

And you and I, with all our knowledge—are we doing any different?

The soul of the calf-worshipper, who with all other human beings is God's child, is thus seeking, though blindly, its Father-Mother Creator-Sustainer. Can anyone dare say it won't find what it seeks? Won't we say, instead, that according to the immutable law, "he that seeks finds" (Matthew 7:8)?

No Need to Convert Others

The moment anyone really comes to recognize this absolute Truth—that one Spirit, the Father-Mother Creator-Sustainer, being made manifest in the Son, always lives at the center of all human beings—they'll know they can stop being anxious about bringing others into the teaching. If your friend, husband or wife, brother or sister, doesn't see Truth as you see it, don't try to convert them with arguments. There's no need for you to try to lift up your friends and family with human intellect (so fond of arguing!).

Remember, the Holy Spirit within all of us declares "I ... will draw all men unto myself" (John 12:32). So you can silently lift up this "I" of another's being and the Spirit will draw them up—not unto your own teaching but unto the Christ within.

Keep your own light lifted up by living the victorious life of Spirit. Then remember that your dear ones are an incarnation of that Spirit and keep them silently committed to the care of their own divine Spirit. You can't know what God wants them to do.

If you fully recognize that the God dwelling in you dwells in all human beings, you know that each one's own Lord, the Christ within each one, will make no mistake. The greatest help you can give anyone then is to repeat silently, whenever you think of that person,

> The Holy Spirit lives within you. Our Father-Mother God cares for you and is bringing forth in you that which is your fulfillment to be and do, which is manifesting through you now.

Then let them alone. Be at perfect peace about them and the result will be much better than anything you could have asked for.

If you want to help others who are not yet awakened to this knowledge, center your thoughts on this idea of them: that they are radiating fountains of the All-Perfect. Keep your eye "single" for others, as did the orthodox woman for herself, and Spirit will teach them more in a day than you could in years.

Always keep in mind that each living person in all God's creation is a radiating center of the same perfect One, radiating more or less, depending on their awakening. And if you are aware of your own radiating center, keep your thought focused right there, and the Spirit of the living God will radiate from you in all directions with a mighty power, doing without noise or words the great work of lifting others up.

TRANSCENDENT PRINCIPLE & LOVING PARENT—BOTH

For uncounted ages, humanity has held to the idea of separateness instead of oneness. People have believed themselves separate from God and separate from each other. And even now, when we talk so much about oneness, most teachers of metaphysics are managing still to separate God's children from their loving Father-Mother. How? By saying that while the child may suffer, infinite Mind knows no suffering, and is unaware of the child's suffering. They suggest that we, who are forever a part of the one God, are torn and lacerated, but God, knowing nothing of this, goes on serenely and indifferently.

It's no wonder, then, that many people who experienced their first practical lessons in the gospel of the Christ as liberation and power have, in times of heartache or failures, turned back to their old limited belief of the "judging Father" personality of God.

There's no real reason for us, having recognized God as infinite substance, to be deprived of the familiar loving Presence that's so dear to the human heart.

There's no need for us to separate God as substance from God as loving Parent. They are One. God principle around us is unchanging law, God within as Spirit is tender, loving Father-Mother with compassion for our every sorrow.

Just because in our childhood some of us were forced into narrow puritanical limits that stood for religious belief doesn't mean that now we should fancy ourselves so self-sufficient that we'll never need the sweet communion between Parent and Child. We, the created, who every moment live and move and have our being in the Creator, need the conscious Presence of that Creator. We can't be entirely happy knowing God only as cold, unsympathetic Principle.

Why can't we accept both? Both are true and both are essential to the whole.

God as underlying Substance of all things, as principle, is unchanging and unmoved by the apparent changes of time and sense. God as principle feels no pain and is not moved by the cries of children or adults for help. It's a grand, wonderful thought that this infinite power is forever unchanging—we can feel our being expanding, just with the thought of it!

But there is gospel ("good news") also, and gospel fulfills the law. God is principle *and* individual. Principle becomes individualized the moment it comes to dwell in the human body. It does not change because of pity or sympathy; it always moves into helpfulness when called on and trusted. (Remember, Jesus called God "Daddy.") Focalized within the human body, infinite wisdom and power are manifest as infinite love, with all the warmth and tender helpfulness that implies.

Then, in some way, the indwelling One moves to lift the consciousness of the soul, or Christ child, up to a place of oneness with Principle and Law so that the three: human consciousness (the Son), indwelling Spirit (the Holy Spirit) and Principle (the Creator Source) are One.

The whole business of your Lord (the Spirit Presence unique to your being) is to care for you, love you with an everlasting love, hear your slightest cry, and carry you through the "shadow" times.

If you ask, "Then why doesn't He do it?" remember. You must recognize that Spirit dwelling in you as all Power, resolutely affirming that your God manifests now as all-sufficiency to call it forth into visibility.

God is our present help in time of need, but there must be a recognition of the Presence, a turning away from human efforts, and an acknowledgement of God as the only Power and Presence before that help becomes our experience.

Amen.

SUMMARY

- Behind all the variety of human understandings is one Mind.

- There's no real wall of difference between the various religions or sects, only those that appear because of a limited viewpoint.

- The Holy Spirit within all of us declares "I ... will draw all men unto myself" (John 12:32). So you can help others who are not yet awakened to this knowledge when you silently lift up this "I" of their being—the Spirit will draw them up.

- There's no need for us to separate God as infinite, eternal Substance and Principle from God as loving Parent; they are One. This is because, within the human body, infinite wisdom and power manifest as infinite love, with all the warmth and tender helpfulness that implies.

Books by Emma Curtis Hopkins

- *Class Lessons of 1888 (WiseWoman Press)*
- *Bible Interpretations (WiseWoman Press)*
- *Esoteric Philosophy in Spiritual Science (WiseWoman Press)*
- *Genesis Series 1894 (WiseWoman Press)*
- *High Mysticism (WiseWoman Press)*
- *Self Treatments with Radiant I Am (WiseWoman Press)*
- *The Gospel Series (WiseWoman Press)*
- *Judgment Series in Spiritual Science (WiseWoman Press)*
- *Drops of Gold (WiseWoman Press)*
- *Resume (WiseWoman Press)*
- *Scientific Christian Mental Practice (DeVorss)*

Books about Emma Curtis Hopkins and her teachings

- *Emma Curtis Hopkins, Forgotten Founder of New Thought – Gail Harley*
- *Unveiling Your Hidden Power: Emma Curtis Hopkins' Metaphysics for the 21st Century (also as a Workbook and as A Guide for Teachers) – Ruth L. Miller*
- *Power to Heal: Easy reading biography for all ages – Ruth Miller*

To find more of Emma's work, including some previously unpublished material, log on to:

www.highwatch.org

www.emmacurtishopkins.com

WISEWOMAN PRESS

Vancouver, WA 98665
800.603.3005
www.wisewomanpress.com

Books by Emma Curtis Hopkins

- *Resume*
- *The Gospel Series*
- *Class Lessons of 1888*
- *Self Treatments including Radiant I Am*
- *High Mysticism*
- *Genesis Series 1894*
- *Esoteric Philosophy in Spiritual Science*
- *Drops of Gold Journal*
- *Judgment Series*
- *Bible Interpretations: Series I, thru XXII*

Books by Ruth L. Miller

- *Unveiling Your Hidden Power: Emma Curtis Hopkins' Metaphysics for the 21st Century*
- *Coming into Freedom: Emily Cady's Lessons in Truth for the 21st Century*
- *150 Years of Healing: The Founders and Science of New Thought*
- *Power Beyond Magic: Ernest Holmes Biography*
- *Power to Heal: Emma Curtis Hopkins Biography*
- *The Power of Unity: Charles Fillmore Biography*
- *Power of Thought: Phineas P. Quimby Biography*
- *The Power of Insight: Thomas Troward Biography*
- *The Power of the Self: Ralph Waldo Emerson Biography*
- *Uncommon Prayer*
- *Spiritual Success*
- *Finding the Path*

Books by Ute Maria Cedilla

- *The Mysticism of Emma Curtis Hopkins*
- *Volume 1 Finding the Christ*
- *Volume 2 Ministry: Realizing The Christ One in All*